FROM GRIEF
TO GLORY

ONE MAN'S JOURNEY

BY

RICHARD L. MOOK

ISBN: 1-4140-2321-9 (e-book)
ISBN: 1-4140-2322-7 (Paperback)

This book is printed on acid free paper.

1stBooks — rev. 11/18/03

THIS BOOK IS DEDICATED
IN MEMORY
OF THE ONES WHO HAVE
GONE ON BEFORE ME

Mother (Anna), Father (Dorrance, Sr.), Sister (Mary
Janet), another Mother (Hattie), Brothers (Dorrance,
Jr., and Eugene), Wife (Judy), Daughter (Debbie), and
Son (Richie)

CONTENTS

ACKNOWLEDGMENTS

WITH HEARTFELT THANKS
AND GRATEFUL APPRECIATION

To Linda Lauener for the countless hours spent
in helping me proofread and edit this book

To Shannon Cremonese for compiling the contents
of the book and photographs

FOREWORD

When my brother, Richard, asked me to write the foreword for this book, I thought what an honor and privilege it would be to be part of this book. I was surprised when he first told me he was going to write a book, but as I thought about it, I said to myself, "Richard is the person that could do this. Whenever he makes up his mind to do something, he gives his all in his work and plans."

This book will tell of my brother's life, a life that was not easy as he endured many trials, tribulations, and grief. But through it all, he persevered to go on, even though he did not always understand. Because Richard is a Christian, he knew his life was predestined years ago by our Lord and Saviour (Jeremiah 1:5). He pressed forward to finish the race set before him (II Timothy 4:7).

I often think of Richard as a modern-day Job (a man and a book of the Bible). It is hard to understand all of Job's losses, let alone my brother losing his entire family. Sometimes the pain and heartache was more than even I could handle, let alone how Richard ever did. I did not entirely understand all of it myself, but I knew it was all a part of God's plan for his life. Even under such dire circumstances, I tried to encourage Richard and tell him of God's promise of eternal life in heaven where he would not only see Jesus but once again see his entire family.

I still do not fully understand how so much tragedy and grief could befall one person, let alone my brother. Maybe when we finally get to be with the Lord, we will know. But then it will be all wiped away, for the Father says there will be no more sorrow, sadness, or tears in Heaven (Revelation 21:4). When Richard sees Jesus, he will say it was all worth it because he will be with his Saviour—the same Lord who in the footprints poem carried him and watched over him when he thought he was alone. Then Richard will live with Jesus and his family eternally. They will all be there waiting for him. Richard ran the race, fought a good fight, and kept his faith. He finished the race and will receive his own crown as Jesus promised (II Timothy 4:7).

This book has been in the making for several years and, after hundreds of hours of preparation, it will be done. I think that as family, friends, and people all over read this book that they will be inspired emotionally and spiritually. Many may reap the rewards for it through Jesus. They will be able to look inside themselves and see how Richard has touched their lives through Jesus. As you read this book, you will see that Richard has not only gone through a lot but he has left us a lot, too. I know that you will enjoy reading this book of Richard's life and how he has gone from grief to glory. I pray that you will be inspired by reading it and that your love for the Lord will be that much more for you. God bless you all.

Thank you, Richard, for not only being my brother but my friend, too. Thank you for sharing this book with me and for allowing me to be a part of it. Thank you for letting Jesus do His good will in your

life and for your sharing it. Remember, the best is yet
to come.

I love you.
Your sister, Alice

INTRODUCTION

Every day I thank the Lord for how good He has been to me and I give Him thanks for helping me through all the trials, tribulations, and grief that I have endured throughout my life. I tell Him how great He is and how much I appreciate and love Him. He tells me, "I really appreciate and love you, too. I love to hear your praises, but if you feel that way about Me and think I'm that good, then would you please tell someone else what you think of Me?"

I have told lots of people about Jesus and now I hope to tell many more people about Him by writing this book. I will share with you my own personal testimonies of my life through the stories I tell. I will tell you about the three different phases of my life: where I have been, where I am now, and where I will be in the future. In sharing with you, I will tell you about my life as a boy growing up and the trials that my parents and my family went through. Then I will share with you my own personal trials, tribulations, and grief. I will tell you that today I am a saved* person. I will share with you how I got saved* and what the Lord means to me. Then I will tell you where I am going and what I have to do to get there.

In this book I will tell you that I have lost the nine closest people in my life and how I have overcome this grief and turned it into glory. The nine closest people in my life were: a mother, a sister, my dad, another mother, two brothers, a daughter, my wife, and my son. Eight of these nine people average less than 35 years of age. Not too good of a track record, but it is what I have been dealt. I will try not to write a eulogy about each of my losses. Instead, I would like to share a little about some of them and tell you what they meant to me.

Also in this book I will thank many different people in my life. People who have tried to help me and were role models for me. People who made a big difference in my life. Most of all, I will give thanks to Jesus our Lord and Saviour for His help, understanding, and patience with me. He has been with me through all kinds of trials and tribulations. He has never left me even though I did not always follow Him. I often wonder where else you can treat someone so badly and that person would still love you. Thank you, Jesus, for loving me.

I will tell you about my early beginnings so you will get a chance to know who I am and where I came from. I will share with you how the Lord put some of the right people in my life to help me go through the trials. I will share how I have overcome these obstacles and turned it all into glory for Him. I have been down many times in my life but with the help and patience of the Lord I still persevered and today I am closer to the Lord more than ever.

In this book I will tell you how I got help for my problems and how I overcame my own grief. I will try and give you my ideas on how to help you with your trials and grief, too. The only way is to go right straight through it -and that is just what I did. Take it one day at a time. Remember that JESUS never fails, and it is no secret what GOD can do. Take it to the

Lord in prayer. Read your Bible faithfully. There are many Bible verses that will help you out. One of my favorites and one of the ones that helped me most is Jeremiah 29:11: "For I know the plans I have for you, declares the Lord, plans for a future and a hope."

This is a story about a man named Richard and his plans for a future and a hope. It is about how he overcame adversity and went from grief to glory.

CHAPTER 1

Richard Mook's Family Tree

Most of this chapter was taken from the journals of Dorrance Mook (Richard's father), Lewis Abbott (Richard's uncle and Dorrance's brother-in-law), and Sally Abbott (Richard's aunt, Lewis's sister, And Dorrance's sister-in-law). These journals were written in the 1940's, 1950's, and 1960's. Lewis and Sally are Richard's mother's (Anna) half-brother and sister. Lewis, Sally, and Anna had the same father but different mothers. This will help explain the names of some of the people mentioned in this book.

On a cold winter night on the sixth of November in 1941, Dorrance Mook went upstairs to go to bed in the old farmhouse in Cambridge Springs, Pennsylvania, and told his sons, "It's another boy. You got a little baby brother named Richard." I was born at home, just like the other two sons of Dorrance and Anna Mae Abbott Shellito Mook. My brothers, Dorrance, Jr. and Louis (Eugene) were born in 1937 and 1938, respectively. I usually refer to my brother Dorrance as Jr. and my brother Louis as Gene. We always referred to my brother Louis as Louie until he was in high school and then he decided he wanted to be called Eugene or Gene. It took a long time for me to do this as I had called him Louie for about 12 years. My brother Dorrance is only called Jr. by his brothers and sister and my mom and dad. Everyone else calls him Dorrance. Obviously, he is named after my dad but he never liked to be referred to as Jr.

Louis is named after my adopted grandfather, Lewis Shellito, though the names are spelled differently. How this mix-up happened I don't know for sure. I was told that my dad got it mixed when he had it put on the birth certificate. My dad usually spelled words as they are pronounced. I guess it could go either way. I also have a sister named Alice who was born in 1943. I will talk more about my brothers and sister a little later in the book.

My father, Dorrance, Sr., comes from a family of 14 brothers and sisters. Six of them passed away at birth or shortly thereafter. He was born to Jesse Mook and Henrietta Smock Mook in Guys Mills, Pennsylvania, on February 6, 1907. Jesse was a farmer and concentrated mostly on raising and selling produce at The Market House in Meadville, Pennsylvania. Jesse and Henrietta were both born and raised in Pennsylvania and were married in 1890. They settled in Guys Mills, Pennsylvania, and raised all their children there.

Anna Mae was born to Floyd Abbott and Lizzie Shellito in a rural area called Conneaut Lake, Pennsylvania, on September 1, 1916. Anna's parents were married in 1913 at the Baptist Church in Meadville, Pennsylvania. After Anna's mother died during childbirth in 1918, she was adopted by Lewis Edmund Shellito. Therefore, Anna Mae Abbott became Anna Mae Abbott Shellito.

Anna's adopted father, Lewis E. Shellito, was a constable, veterinarian, and farmer who raised mostly horses. His farm was located west of Conneaut Lake on Geiser Road off Route 285 in Sadsbury Township. (Note: The original dinner bell is still attached to the garage and the house is now used as a hunting camp.)

Lewis Shellito's first cousin, Mary Shellito, owned the farm which she had inherited from her parents and grandparents. Lewis and Mary Shellito then raised Anna together. When Anna was about 18 years old, Lewis Shellito died and the funeral was held on the farm. Anna's biological father, Floyd Abbott, attended the funeral along with Anna's half brother Lewis (Lew) Abbott. This was in November of 1933. In 1934 Mary Shellito died. It was then that Anna went to stay with her biological father Floyd Abbott and family in Edinboro, Pennsylvania. Floyd was remarried and now had other children. Anna stayed until September of 1935 and then took a job working for the Griffin family on Pine Street in Meadville, Pennsylvania. It was told that her earnings were about $5.00 a week which, at that time, was not too bad of wage for domestic type work.

The most confusing and coincidental part of Anna's family tree is this: Anna's grandmother (Lizzie's mother), Mary Robison who came from Titusville, Pennsylvania, was employed by Mary Shellito on the farm in Conneaut Lake. Mary Robison was not married when Lizzie was born. Hoping for a better life for her daughter, she gave her up for adoption to Mary Shellito. Therefore, at the age of 6 Lizzie Robison became Lizzie Shellito. This happened around 1899. Then Anna Mae Abbott was adopted by Lewis Shellito in 1918 and, along with the help of

Mary Shellito, they raised Anna. Oddly enough, that makes Mary Shellito to be Anna's grandmother (my great-grandmother) and Lewis Shellito her father (my grandfather). That means that my mother and grandmother were raised by Lewis and Mary Shellito, who are my grandfather and great-grandmother, respectively. I hope that this makes sense to those who would be interested about the partial family tree of the Richard Mook family. This will give you a short version and view of Richard's immediate family.

CHAPTER 2

The Early Years

The war had started shortly after I was born and, even though the Depression was over, the hard times continued. My father had already moved 3 or 4 times since being married in 1936. Work was hard to find despite a war going on. Many things were rationed and many items were hard to buy. My dad pretty much lived off the farm for our food. Things got so bad that my dad decided to enlist in the army. When he went down to the recruiting and enlistment station and they found out that he had 3 children, they sent him home immediately. They said he had too many dependents and to go home and take care of his family.

My father finally found work in Meadville, Pennsylvania, at the Channel Lock Company. This is a factory that makes the channel lock pliers that are known throughout the world. He also found work at the Hookless Fastener Company, which is known throughout the world, too. It makes mostly zippers. These two companies, along with the Dad's Dog Food Company, employ many people in this area.

Now that my dad had a job, things were going better and my parents were expecting another child. So the Mooks decided to move to a larger place. This area was called Sagerstown, Pennsylvania. It is where the Woodcock Dam was built and is a beautiful area today. Things were going along well until the day we moved. This is where I caused a big problem for the family. I do not understand how I ever did this nor was it ever explained to me, but somehow I decided I was thirsty and found a jar with something in it that looked like water, so I decided to take a drink. What a mistake! It was gasoline. I could not have drunk very much of it but it made me deathly ill. With my brother, Louie, holding me, my dad raced me to the Meadville General Hospital in his Model A Ford. It was told that he did not stop for anything. Of course, there was not a lot of traffic like there would be today. The doctors said that my dad got me to the hospital just in time. They had to pump my stomach out and watch me for a few days.

We did not live in Sagerstown too long as it was on a big hill and during that winter my dad had trouble making it up the hill with the old Model A. We then moved to Edinboro in the summer of 1943. My sister, Alice, was born here. We lived there for a couple of years and then my dad finally had a chance to buy a farm in Cambridge Springs, Pennsylvania. So that is where we moved next. It was a pretty nice little farm, and I had lots of fun there as a little boy growing up. It was there that I learned to ride a two-wheeled bike. I couldn't get up on the bike because it was too high. The 26-inch bike was for my two older brothers and was too big for me to get on, so I would put the bike alongside of the hay wagon and get on it from there. I would then push off the wagon to get it started and away I would go. It was fun riding it but when I stopped to get off, I had trouble. So I just jumped off and hoped I didn't get hurt. I was young and didn't think about getting hurt. I have always wanted a bicycle of my own but, even to this day, I do not have one of my own.

My dad raised different kinds of animals on the farm and, even though he was working, he still dabbled in fruit and produce. Even at a young age, I found out what work was as I had my own little jobs to do. I had to feed the chickens, put grass into the pigpen, and find clover to feed to the rabbits. Even though I thought of it as work then, today I look at it as having fun and part of growing up. Since my brothers were older, they had to do the barn work but I would help out, too.

We had to make our own fun. I remember building a little dam in the creek so we could have a swimming hole. Then we built a little clubhouse that was just for us brothers. I talk like I did a lot of the damming of the creek and the building of the clubhouse, but my brothers did most of the work. Even though we were just 8, 6, and 4, we did lots of unimaginable things. Like I said, when you live where we did and didn't have other kids to play with, you made up your own things. While most things seemed like fun and games for me, my dad and mom had lots of problems.

CHAPTER 3

Alice Has Problems

In 1945, while still living in Cambridge Springs, Pennsylvania, my mom and dad noticed that Alice was having a hard time learning to walk. They noticed that she was always leaning and falling to one side. The boys did not have that trouble when we were growing up and learning to walk. Remember, we were all born at home and had never been to a hospital or even seen a doctor. Mostly this was due to the fact that my dad did not have hospital insurance and did not make enough money to pay the doctor bills. As I mentioned before, he basically made his living off the farm. My parents sensed this time, though, that something was very wrong and they took Alice to a doctor. The news was not very good, and they had to take her to other specialists. The prognosis was not very good there, either. She was diagnosed with curvature of the spine. She would have to have several operations and be in the hospital and have physical therapy for a long time.

Several problems arose from Alice's problem. My parents would never be able to pay all of the doctor and hospital bills. On top of this, there was no guarantee that Alice would ever walk again! In the meantime, she had started walking but her spine was so curved that when she walked one hand drug the floor. She seemed to crawl more than walk. I can

8

remember, even at my young age, that people would look and stare. It was bad enough to stare at us boys but now people stared even more at my sister. However, Alice didn't seem to have much trouble getting around, even with this severe handicap. It did not seem to bother her even with people staring and kids making fun. I was not bothered by it too much, either, but I'm quite sure that my brothers, and certainly my parents, were. The irony of this is that Alice probably got into more things than the boys did. (Ha, Ha) Dad and mom did recognize the fact that she could not be like this for the rest of her life, so after several doctor visits and consultations, they finally gave permission for her to have an operation to straighten out her spine and worry about paying the bills later.

This operation was something new and had not been performed many times. Alice had to have lots of x-rays before the operation. It was then that the doctors found out that she had 6 extra ribs. These extra ribs were part of the reason for her leaning to one side and making her spine curve to one side. This was extremely detrimental at her young age while she was starting to grow. This was a lot of the reason for the curving of the spine, but not the only one. These ribs would have to be removed first.

The operation took place at the Zim Zim Hospital in Erie, Pennsylvania. This is a hospital that specializes in "crippled children." The operation took several hours and many doctors to complete. It consisted of taking out the extra ribs and using these ribs, plus taking bones from both legs, and putting these into her back to straighten it out. The operation was very difficult and extremely dangerous, especially in 1944/45. I cannot imagine this operation taking place now, much less then.

During this difficult and life-threatening operation, Alice would be under anesthetic for a very long time. The operation would consist of cutting under each arm, removing the extra ribs, saving the rib bones, and then sewing that up. Next the surgeons would cut both legs from the knees down and take out bones, saving them to use later. They then sewed up her legs. The next part of the operation was to cut down her back from her neck to the lowest part of her back. They then fused some of the bones taken from her ribs and legs to straighten out her back. I cannot explain it like a doctor would, but the operation had to be work that only GOD could have directed. Only GOD could have guided the surgeons' hands as they performed this difficult task. It would take a long time before this operation was deemed a successful one.

Alice was in the hospital for months recovering, and then more months of physical therapy. It was almost two years before the operation was considered successful and she was able to walk "normal." As I look back on it today, it was surely a miracle. As Alice was growing up, she was told that she probably could never have children and, even if she could, it would be best not to. It could cost her life if she were to have children. This did not seem to bother her after she married because now she has two daughters. She did have serious problems delivering her second daughter and almost died. She and her husband then decided to have no more children. They were blessed with two children and were thankful to the Lord for that.

At this time in our lives we did not belong to a church. I do not believe that my dad was saved*, but my mother was. She attended church with the neighbors who would stop and pick her up. My mother, along with many other church people, did a lot a praying that Alice would be healed and that she would have a successful operation. It would take a miracle from God for Alice to be able to walk "normal."

Even though I was too young to understand the seriousness of all this, today it is the first recognizable miracle that I relate to my family. There may have been others, but this is the one that I relate to myself. Every time I look at my sister, I can't help but remember when her arm drug the floor as she walked. Today it would be almost impossible to notice that she had any difficulties in walking or had any operations at all. She gets around and does most things better than I do. What a blessing! I give thanks to the LORD every time I think about her or when I see her, even though we seldom talk about the ordeal.

I personally think Alice was babied a little along the way, but she took her licks right along with us boys. Of course, you have to remember that she was the only girl in our family so my dad and mom favored her a little and were very protective of her. Today, Alice has been married to her husband, Lloyd, for 42 years and has two daughters, Anna and Tammy. They have seven grandchildren and four great-grandchildren. She has been blessed with good health and has had little problem with her back or spine. The Lord has watched over her for many years and she is extremely thankful. I, too, say thank you, Jesus, for watching over her.

CHAPTER 4

My Mother Passes Away

It is in the summer of 1946 now. Alice is walking and getting around pretty well. My mom is going to have another baby. Dad is still working on the farm. Things are going along all right now, but that doesn't last for long.

As winter came along and Thanksgiving was approaching, my mom went into labor with the new baby. My brothers, my sister, and I were all born at home, but this time my mother was having difficulty and was hemorrhaging. She had to be taken to a hospital in Greenville, Pennsylvania. My brothers both woke up and went with my dad. I cannot understand and do not know what state of mind my dad was in, but he left my sister and me home alone. I guess he was thinking of getting mom to the hospital and my brothers would not stay at home and insisted on going. It was told to me that they just jumped into the back seat, and my dad didn't even know they were there until he was almost to the hospital. Then it was too late to go back. I guess he felt that my sister and I were both sound asleep and he would be gone for only a little while. My sister and I woke up during the night and discovered that we were by ourselves. We went downstairs and got into our mom and dad's bed and started crying, trying to figure out what was happening. We were only three and five years old at the time.

My sister and I had not been up for too long when we heard a car pull into the driveway. It was my dad and brothers. As they came into the house, I can remember that they were all crying. It was then that my dad explained to us that our mother had died and so had our baby sister who had only lived a few hours. The baby was named Mary Janet after the Mary (Shellito) who adopted my grandmother and helped raise my mother. My mother was only 30 years old. Her death was attributed to hemorrhaging during childbirth.

Some of the only memories that I have of my mother are of the night she passed away and of the days following at the funeral. They are not very good memories, but still they are all I have of her today. I do remember some friends of my mom and dad coming to our house and talking to our dad. We all got on our knees and they prayed for my dad and our family. As they were leaving, they gave my dad a decorative cardboard with some sayings written in some kind of sparkly stuff. The sayings were displayed on the walls of our house until my dad passed away. When my dad passed away, I got one of the cardboard sayings. It said, THE WAY OF THE CROSS LEADS HOME. I still have this saying on the original cardboard, and it now hangs on the wall in my house today. The other saying was JESUS NEVER FAILS. These two sayings have been instrumental in helping me throughout my life. I often recite these sayings during difficult times in my life. They will always have a place in my heart. These sayings were given to my dad by the Butterfield family who were friends of my parents. I have not had any contact with this family throughout the years, but I see the name Butterfield on some of the markers in the Guys Mills cemetery where my mother is buried.

It would be hard to imagine where my dad was at this time in his life or the thoughts that my brothers might have had. My sister was too young to understand the loss of our mother and, at that time, it did not really set in with me as I was only five years old. Obviously, my dad took it pretty hard.

It really was not until after the loss of my daughter and then the loss of my wife that I could begin to understand the position my dad was in and could sense some of his feelings throughout my years growing up. I respect my dad very much, especially when I think of all the grief he went through and how he still went on with his life without doing much complaining. His situation was different from mine, mostly because he had four children yet to raise. What a responsibility that must have been! I still had my son when my losses occurred, but he was raised and pretty much on his own. The loss of my son was not easy for me, either, but I can now better understand the reasoning behind my dad's life and various decisions that he made.

My dad did not talk about my mom too much, but sometimes I would look at him when he was thinking to himself and I could see the pain and sadness in his eyes. My brothers were a little older and, therefore, more attached to our mom. They never talked too much about her, either, but I could see that they missed her very much. I am thankful for many things in my life, but I still cannot help but wonder how much different all our lives would have been if my mother had lived.

Now, my dad was left alone to try and raise four children. He had just lost his wife and baby daughter. It was very difficult to find someone to watch us while he tried to deliver his produce and make some kind of living. He still had bills to pay and a family to feed. He had several "housekeepers" in to watch us, but none would stay long. I would have to think that there was no pay involved, and it was probably just for room and board. Watching four kids for nothing would be hard to do, but he found several ladies who tried. Jr. and Louie could pretty well take care of themselves, but Alice and I were "shipped out" to other people that my dad knew. One of these was a family by the name of Crosby. It was while Alice and I were staying with them during the spring of 1947 that she fell off the swings and injured her back again. She had to be taken to the doctor. After contacting my father and learning of the severity of the injury, Alice was once again taken to the Zim Zim Hospital in Erie. Her back had been fractured and she had to be put in a body cast and in some kind of traction. She was in the hospital for the next several months. During that time, my dad was trying to divide his time between going to the hospital to see Alice almost every day, delivering his produce, and trying to take care of the rest of us. This was pretty hard to do, especially when he could not get anyone to watch the rest of us kids.

While Alice was in the hospital, I had to stay with my Uncle Ern (actually, my great-uncle). What a nightmare that was! Uncle Ern was probably in his 70's, maybe even his 80's, and he was a confirmed bachelor, having never been married. He lived in an old rooming house in Meadville, Pennsylvania. It was not very good for me to stay with him, but my dad was running out of options, I guess. Old Ern was an alcoholic and would take me to the bars with him. He promised my dad that he would not go to the bars while he watched me, but that didn't last for long. Lots of time I can remember crying and his trying to cover my mouth with the pillow to stop me from crying. After my dad came to pick me up, on the way home he asked if I liked staying with Uncle Ern. It was then that I told him how badly he treated me. I do not think that my dad believed me 100 percent, but I never had to stay with old Uncle Ern again.

Believe it or not, I did learn some valuable lessons while staying with Uncle Ern. By staying with him at such a young age, I could see what drinking alcohol could do to a person. I can still see him staggering around, even messing his pants, and really not having any idea what he was doing. To this day, I have never had a drink in my life, not even a sip of beer. I literally cannot stand even the smell of beer. I also learned that chewing tobacco was nasty, too. Uncle Ern chewed Mail Pouch tobacco, and one day he offered me some. For whatever reasons, I decided to try it and took some. I put it in my mouth and started chewing. I never remember him spitting, so I didn't either. You can guess the rest of the story. I became sicker than a dog. I was never so sick in my entire life. Hence, I do not use any tobacco products today either. Maybe something good did come from my staying with old Uncle Ern.

Jr. and Louis were in school during this time. Alice was in the hospital, and that left only me to be taken care of. Since my dad did not want me to stay with Uncle Ern anymore, he decided to send me to school with my brothers. I was only five and, at that time, there was no pre-school or kindergarten in our area. (I consider myself as being the first kid in our area to go to preschool/kindergarten, possibly the first in the county or the state of Pennsylvania.) My dad did not receive too much flak about this because the school was a one-room schoolhouse and the one and only teacher the school had was our neighbor. Her name was Miss Wycoff. She was a nice older lady who had never married and helped our family out a lot when we were young and growing up. She was a big help to my dad, even though she did not "babysit" us as such. She did pick us up and take us to school in her Model A Ford and then bring us back home. Lots of times she would have something for us to eat at lunchtime. We mostly took different fruits and vegetables to school for lunch, as that was what we had on the farm.

Miss Wycoff taught all four of us children in school. She stayed on until Alice was in the first grade and then retired around 1950. I am not sure but I was told that this was her 50th year of teaching and that she started teaching in 1899. After we moved in 1950, my family lost track of her. She was already up in years and I do not know how much longer she lived. I do not know of any other relatives she had except her brother, and he never married either. To contact anyone from her family would be hard to do today. Miss Wycoff played a big part in helping our family and teaching us as young children. I have many fond memories of Miss Wycoff and that little one-room schoolhouse. Thank you, Miss Wycoff, and God bless your soul.

That little school brings forth lots of memories. It was heated by a wood/coal stove and we had to take turns bringing the fuel into the school every day. Miss Wycoff would start the fire every morning and my brothers would help because we were the first ones there. We had to go to the neighbors every morning to get water to use for that day. We used to play ball at recess time and even go swimming in the little creek behind the school. Can you imagine going swimming in the water hole behind the school at recess time? Of course, I didn't do too much since I was the youngest kid in the school. We were even allowed to take our sleds to school and sled ride at recess and lunch break during the winter months. There was this little hill beside the school, and we used to sled ride there lots of days.

During the spring we would play baseball a lot. We even went to a neighboring school and played against their team. I do not remember playing on the team but I do remember my brothers playing. Years later, my brothers would tell stories about playing baseball against the other school teams, but I think some of their stories were exaggerated. I could not understand how they would get to the other schools to play ball. Louie said that Miss Wycoff took them in her Model A Ford. How they ever got enough kids in her old Ford to make up a baseball team still puzzles me to this day.

I can remember using the wrong water glass and Miss Wycoff reprimanding me by smacking my hands. We each had our own glass to drink out of, but I would just take the first one I saw and could reach. I did not care what glass I had. I just wanted a drink.

I had so much fun because I did not have to do very much. I only attended school there in the winter of 1946 and the spring of 1947. Then I went into the first grade in the fall at the grade school in Sagerstown, Pennsylvania. The name of the little one-room schoolhouse was the Woodcock Schoolhouse. It is still there today and some family made a little home out of it. I always stop and take a glance at it when I am out that way. When my son was with me, I would tell him about the "good old days" at the school. He could not believe that I went to school there and some of the stories that I told him about the schoolhouse.

CHAPTER 5

Lots of Changes

It is now the spring of 1947. I remember that day when we got home from school and my dad had a family meeting. He did not call it a family meeting, though. He would just say, "Okay, guys, listen up." He did not waste too much time with idle conversation and got right to the point. He said, "You know that I've been having trouble finding ladies to come in and watch you, and I have to have some kind of order here. I'm going to have to put Jr. in charge. You will have to listen to him and follow his directions to a "T" if we are to stay together. When Jr. says something, it's the same as if I said it." A pretty strong statement, but we all knew what our dad meant, and he was dead serious. There was no discussion.

We were now ages nine, seven, five, and Alice was three. What a responsibility for a nine-year old. I know that this would seem impossible to most people, but you have to understand that Jr. was quite mature for his age. Even at nine he was a no-nonsense type of kid. Jr. grabbed hold and took care of us in a pretty adult-like fashion. He was not bossy nor did he try to tell us what to do all the time. He just did what he had to do and relayed to us what dad expected us to do. I will talk about Jr. in more detail later in the book.

That situation went along for a while until someone reported my dad to the social service authorities. My dad was told that he could not have a nine-year old watching the rest of us, even though Jr. was mature for his age and did a pretty good job of taking care of us. They told my dad that social services would have to take us away and would have temporary custody of us. After several meetings, social services said that they had found a home for each one of us, including Alice with her physical problems. My dad asked if they meant separate places for all of us and they said yes. They could not find anyone to take all four of us. I can remember dad telling them that we would not be separated and that we were not going anyplace. His actual statement was, "Over my dead body will you separate my children."

MOM & DAD 1947

A few days later in late May, we got the surprise of our lives when we came home from school. Louie was the first one to walk into the house. He did a 180 degree turn and came running out the door, yelling, "There's an old lady in there!" Excuse that expression, but that is exactly what he said. (I know that this was not very good manners, but that is a term that lots of kids used for any adult that was much older than any of us. At that time, 40 was old to us.) We thought that Louie was playing a joke on us and not telling the truth. Jr. then took a peek in the window, and he came back and told the same story (except for the "old lady" part). Jr. and Louie would not go in and check things out, so they sent me in to get the scoop on what was happening. One of those "Let Richie try it!" I guess I did not know any better, so in the house I went. Sure enough, there was someone in there. An older lady was fixing something at the sink. "Does my dad know you're here? What are you doing here? Where's my dad at?" I asked all these questions and probably more. I did not give her a chance to answer back. When I finally quit asking questions and gave her a chance to answer, she told me that she was there to watch us kids until my dad got someone else to do it. Then I proceeded to ask 20 more questions, and she answered most of them. Finally, Jr. and Louie came to the door because I had been in there for so long. They called me back outside and began to question me. Everything seemed to be on the up-and-up, but they decided that they were not going to go inside until dad came home. We just stayed outside until dad came home a few hours later. Just as soon as he pulled in the driveway, we all ran to tell him the news. He did not seem surprised, though. He said that she was there to watch over us, just as the lady said.

Then we had one of our little family talks where daddy just told us what was happening. This time the talk involved the lady, too. The talk went something like this:

"This is the lady who will be watching over you. She will tell you what to do, what chores each of you have, when it's time to work or time to play, when it's time to eat and when to go to bed. In the short version, she is in charge and will make all the decisions when I'm not here. Do you all understand?" I cannot remember any of us asking any questions and we all nodded our heads in agreement. Once the three of us boys were outside together, we had a different line to say, or at least Louie did. He said, "I'm not going to listen to her. She's not our mother." Being the calm and more mature one, Jr. said, "We have to listen or dad said they will split us up and take us away." I really did not know what to say, but I usually agreed with Jr.

It was good to have someone to fix us breakfast, pack our lunches for school, and make us dinner in the evening. The lady even helped me get ready for school and made sure I was wearing something halfway decent. Jr. and Louie could pretty well do for themselves, but I had trouble picking out my clothes even though I did not have many choices. She still made us toe the line, though. We all had to do our chores before we could play. She wasn't mean but would say that this is what your dad wants you to do today, and we pretty well did what she said. I thought that I had a lot of rough work to do and not very much time to play. Of course as I look back on it today, I really did not have that much to do since I was only five at that time. What can a five-year old do? Of course, as I got older I had to work just like my brothers. To give you an example: When I was 8 I could milk a cow by myself and get three gallons of milk in five minutes. Everyone had to do his part, including me. I had to cut and put the corn into shocks, and the same thing with the wheat and oats. We put all the hay up loose by making stacks and then loaded it on the wagon. Next, we transferred the hay to the mow in the barn. Back-breaking work for a young boy. I learned at a young age that we had to work together to stay together. There were always plenty of chores to do. My dad made sure of that.

The summer went by, and then it was time for me to go to the big school. I would be in the first grade. This was in September of 1947. It certainly was different from going to the little one-room schoolhouse. Here, the teacher made me behave all the time. That was hard for me to do since it seemed like I was always getting into trouble. There were lots more kids in the class, and it was only the first grade! What did they expect? I did not like to sit all day and was easily distracted. I suppose I acted up some to get attention, but I seemed to get the wrong attention, especially from the teachers. They were sending notes home about my behavior all the time. There will be more about grade school a little later in the book.

At home it was time for another talk with dad and the lady we now called Hattie. Dad had another surprise for us. This time he told us that he and Hattie were going to be married. The marriage occurred that same September. Louie once again became obstinate and said he wasn't going to call her mom. Dad said that was okay, he didn't have to. Jr. did not voice his opinion either way, and I did not know any better. She was like a mom to me, so I called her mom. Actually, I called her mommy. Even though Jr. and Louie knew our real mother better than Alice and I, they eventually called her mom, too. Hattie treated us all like her own. I never refer to her as anything but mommy. She was now married to my dad and it looked like she was going to be around for a long time. She was to be my mom for many years.

When Alice came home from the hospital, I told her that we had a new mom. This was the only mother that Alice and I ever really knew. After a while Jr. and Louie were calling her mom, too. Louie was the most reluctant to do so. She helped raise us and we all considered her our mom.

Hattie (mommy) had two children of her own. Her daughter, Marie, lived in State Village, Pennsylvania. She was grown and lived in a girls' home there. Over the years we would visit with her and she eventually moved in with us in Edinboro. This was in the late 50's or early 60's. There will be more about Marie later.

Mom also had a son named Raymond. He stayed with us for a while in 1947/48 and then went to help the neighboring farmer as a hired hand. He was a little older than Jr. and wanted to be more on his own, even though he was only about 16. My dad and Ray did not always see eye to eye. He never referred to my dad as father and told him, "You're not my father and you can't tell me what to do." My dad's reply was, "I may not be your father, but you will listen to what I have to say as long as you are under my roof and in my house." Over the next several years Ray worked for several farmers in the area and then moved away to Texas. We have not heard from him in over 35 years. I remember him being a loner and wanting to be on his own. To my knowledge, he never married. Because mom's two children were older than we were and mostly on their own, she put most of her attention into raising us. My mommy was married to my dad until his death in 1964. They were married for 17 years. She surely was a blessing from heaven. If it were not for this mom, there would be no telling where we would be today. God bless and thank you, mommy.

Things were going along pretty well for us now. Dad had someone to watch us kids and we were all together. All of us boys were in school and mom just had to watch Alice. My dad still made a living off the farm selling produce and raising some farm animals. We did not have very much but we were all together. At that time in our lives, that was the most important thing to my father and now to my mom.

To be perfectly honest and blunt, we were considered extremely poor by anyone's opinion, and the family barely got by. We always had something to eat. We usually ate a variety of fruits, vegetables, produce, and other things that my dad raised on the farm. Most all of our meat came from our own animals. We never had candy, pop, ice cream, and things like that. I guess that was probably best for us, though. We usually took fruit and vegetables to school, even for our lunch. The other kids would make fun of our lunches, but I do not think I ever saw any other kids at lunchtime eating apples, pears, strawberries, blackberries, and peaches. My mother canned just about any fruit or vegetable that you could name and then some. The other kids would always ask where we got all that stuff, especially the kids that came from the city. At that time they did not have the free lunches and government assistance programs like they do today.

The clothing situation was a whole new ballgame. Most of the clothing we wore was used. My dad would have people give him old clothes as he was delivering his produce. My dad was not bashful and would ask for anything that he could see would help the family survive. It seemed like Louie and Jr. always got first pick, and I wore what they couldn't or what was considered their used hand-me-downs. Somehow they never seemed to have the right sizes for me. Finding clothes for my sister wasn't easy either, and she ended up wearing many of the boys' clothes, like jeans and T-shirts. We laugh about it today and give Alice the distinction of being the first girl ever to wear boys' Levis, pants, and T-shirts. As you well know, ladies and girls wearing men's and boys' Levis, pants, and T-shirts is a multi-billion dollar business and it all started with my sister. (Ha, Ha)

We knew we did not have as much as most of the other kids and families, but we were a little oblivious to it all and just thought it was a way of life. I guess you could say that we did not have a lot of goodies or treats to eat, like chips and pop, but it was a treat for us to go once a year to Conneaut Lake Park for an ice cream.

We were made fun of and picked on almost every day, especially at school. Even the teachers were a part of it. After having Miss Wycoff as a teacher, the next four or five years was all downhill for me as far as my teachers were concerned. The teachers used me as the example of what not to be. I remember the teachers would put me up in front of the class and ask the other kids if they wanted to be like me. They would say, "Do you want to be poor, dirty, stupid, and have nothing like this kid?" I do know one thing, though. It would not happen in today's schools and society.

I remember that first year when my dad was called to school because the teachers thought something was wrong with me because I was so slow and acted up all the time. I did not know my ABC's and could not count to 10 or write my name as I went into first grade. With my first mom gone and my dad trying to keep everything going, there was not much time to teach me my ABC's or any of the things to prepare you for the first grade. My dad told them that's what they had school for. The preschool that I was in was not for teaching me anything. It was a way for someone to watch me or babysit me, as I said earlier. In spite of all this, they put me into the second grade. I guess they thought I must have learned something or they just wanted to get rid of me.

It was not much better in the second grade. Being the lowest and poorest kid on the block, coupled with poor clothes and no friends, did not help me any. Even the teachers continued to pick on me (us). The teacher still put me up in front of the class as an example of what not to be. She would use me for the inspection kid. She said it was bad enough that I did not dress very well but I did not keep very clean either. Her actual statement was that I had "ring around the collar". Then she would parade the other kids around to see for themselves. I suppose I was not the cleanest kid in school, but I do not know why they always put me on display. I washed up the best that I could under the circumstances. We did not have running water or an inside bathroom, and we had to heat all our water on a wood stove. All our water had to be brought in from outside and then heated on the stove. It was most difficult in the winter. We used a big metal tub to take a bath in and that was usually on Sunday nights. I was pretty clean on Monday morning for school, but the rest of the week got continually worse. We had to heat an enormous amount of water for us four kids and mom and dad.

During the week we had to wash up in a wash pan and use just a washcloth. I am almost reluctant to tell you that we had a pecking order in taking a bath— dad, mom, Jr., Gene, and then me. Here I was last again! Mommy would wash Alice because she had difficulty in trying to reach around to do her back because of her back and spine operations. I guess that is why I had so many "rings around my collar."

On top of all this, the teacher said I had some sort of "germs" and used me as an example to the rest of the kids. She and the school nurse took swabs from my mouth and put them under their own microscope so everyone could see my "germs." That certainly did not make me the most popular kid in the class. I have had many physical examinations since then, and no doctor has ever said I had anything contagious. I guess "whatever it was" went away as I got older, even though I was never in the hospital or under any doctor's care that I can remember. I will never forget the embarrassment and shame I suffered because of the cruelty of that teacher and nurse. To this day, I cannot figure out why they singled me out like that. I cannot imagine all this happening today at school with all the lawsuits flying around. Today they sue over your right of just saying The Lord's Prayer in school. What would they do in my case? The lawyers would have a field day. Boy, times sure have changed.

In the summer of 1949 Alice went back into the hospital yet again. Her bones were not healing just right and she had to be put in a cast again. I remember how she was looking forward to being in the first grade that fall. Miss Wycoff had stayed on just so she could have Alice in the first grade. The day before school was supposed to start, she came home from the hospital. She got her vaccination that same day and off to school she went! I was now in the third grade, but things were not too much better because the same kids moved up a grade with me and did not treat me any better. The teachers had wanted to hold me back in second grade because my vision was not too good and the glasses I had did not seem to do the job. I had had these glasses for several years and they were not the right prescription for me at that time. The doctor who had operated on my eyes years before had obtained them for me and my dad had not taken me back since. When the school told him that I could not see very well, he then got in touch with the Lions Club and they fixed me up with better ones. That certainly helped and I could see much better now.

I have had problems with my eyes since birth and had them operated on at a young age. It was bad enough that I could not see well but, to compound the problem, the other kids made fun of me because I wore glasses. I was constantly getting into fights trying to defend myself, and the outcome would inevitably be broken glasses. Thank the Lord for the Lions Club furnishing my glasses for a number of years. Many times the glasses were used ones (previously owned), but they were closer to the right prescription and I was able to see better. I am still grateful to the Lions Club for getting me my first correct pair of glasses and for keeping me in glasses for a number of years. With better glasses I did better in my schoolwork but still barely made it according to my teachers. They did move me on to the fourth grade, though. Once again, things took a bad turn.

CHAPTER 6

Things Take a Turn for the Worse

It is now the summer of 1950 and I am going into the fourth grade. Things are not going too well for my mom and dad. With all the bills coming in over the last few years, my dad was not able to keep up with everything since he did not have insurance of any kind. With my sister, Alice, being in the hospital off and on for almost two years, my eye operations, the deaths of my mom and baby sister, and the Lord knows what else, the bills became totally overwhelming. My dad had to borrow money from the state of Pennsylvania just to keep a roof over our heads and some food in our mouths. In 1950 I guess you just did not go bankrupt and have all your bills taken care of, like today. You just moved on with your life, carrying your load of debt.

My dad had to sell all of his cattle and livestock and give the monies from the proceeds to the state. Of course, this still did not satisfy all the money he owed so the state of Pennsylvania sold my dad's farm and we had to move within 30 days after the sale. Even though the farm was not much, it was all that my dad had and he owned it 100% free and clear after working all his life. Now to have it all taken away from him with the stroke of a pen was quite a blow to him and his pride. Naturally he was concerned about our future, but he was ever so thankful that we were still all together. He said, "We can always get another farm, but my family will not be split up." He wrote such a letter stating the same to the State of Pennsylvania. I have a copy of that letter and would have shared it with the reader but it is too hard and emotional for me to do so.

Though the bills were enormous, quite a few of them were taken care of. My eye doctor wrote all his bills off and, as I said before, the Lions Club provided my glasses for a number of years. My mom and baby sister's hospital and funeral expenses were never quite paid for. Think for a moment about how much the bills for Alice's operations, hospital stays, and therapy would have amounted to. Remember that she was in and out of the hospital for over two years with extended stays for months at a time. I would guess that the bills would have been in the hundreds of thousands of dollars, even in the late 40's. When my dad asked the Zim Zim Hospital and all their doctors how much the bills were, they replied, "Zero, nothing!"

The Zim Zim Hospital is owned by an organization called the Masons. They took care of everything. My dad would never have been able to pay the bills in his time or mine. It was a miracle that the operation was a success, and the bills being paid for was too good to be true. Thank you, Jesus, for her healing and the Masons for taking care of her bills.

The reason my dad lost the farm was mostly due to the fact that he visited Alice in the hospital almost every day and, thus, was not able to work much or even sell his produce. Then the borrowing from the state just to get enough to live on was the eventual downfall. I know that Alice loves our father just as much as the boys do, but I do not think she really understands about all the time dad spent with her in the hospital and what all he gave up to visit with her almost every day. All of this, along with the devastating loss of his wife and baby daughter, took a tremendous toll on him. I respected my dad very much in all that he did for me personally. Even more so, I respected the fact that he never gave up and he put his family ahead of everything, even keeping the farm that he loved so dearly. Whenever I speak of dad taking care of his family, I do not mean so much material-wise but keeping us together as a family unit. Even though our family did not have much and was considered extremely poor by almost any standards, my father died knowing that his most important accomplishment in his life was keeping our family together. During difficult times in my own life, I think about how my dad hung in there and weathered the storms. I think I have never been as destitute as my dad—and he made it! So can I.

In 1950 we were on the road again, this time to Harmansburg, Pennsylvania. For me that meant another school and new kid on the block again. I do not remember too much about fourth grade there. I know that we lived on a big farm and were supposed to get free rent. My dad tried to start up a dairy herd with a guy named Archie Konsley, but that did not pan out because my dad was not able to purchase enough cattle of his own to share and operate with Archie. So we moved again, this time to Linesville, Pennsylvania. I finished out fourth grade there at Graham School. The new kid again, I was still being picked on in school, mostly by bigger kids in the grades ahead of me. I was big enough now to take care of kids my age, but not the ones two or three years older. My brothers seemed to fare better since they were big for their ages. Jr. and Louie were extremely strong and could pretty well take care of themselves. The problem was that they were several years ahead of me in school, so they were not there to help me. I had to defend myself most of the time, so I soon learned to take care of myself. I told my dad and brothers about the other kids picking on me and they told me, "Like the song 'A Boy Named Sue', you had better be able to take care of yourself and, remember, we won't always be there when you get into a fight or run into trouble." That advice prepared me for other obstacles in my life as well.

I do not remember too much at the Graham School either, except that my teacher's name was Mrs. Rea. I only went to school there for half of the year. Then we moved again for the beginning of fifth grade to Edinboro, Pennsylvania. Believe it or not, it was another one-room schoolhouse and was located at a four corners called Franklin Center, Pennsylvania. (I thought all the one-room schoolhouses were either torn down or outlawed by this time.) We had to use the outhouse but, this time at least, we had a pump for water and did not have to go to the neighbors to get it. There was a big wood stove in the back of the room that was used for heating. The students had to take turns bringing in wood and coal from the shed to keep the fire going. Who would think of a school in 1951 with no bathroom, no water, and no furnace? It was bad enough that we did not have an indoor bathroom or running water, but we still had to use a round potbelly stove like the one in our house. I guess I had gotten used to the nice things at the other schools and was spoiled by now. I had fun at this school, though. We were allowed to bring our sleds to school and at recess and lunchtime we would go sledding at the hill up from the school. I still had trouble with most of the kids at the school since I was the new kid again. I was convinced by now that it was not just me and my personality which caused them to pick on me. I knew that it had to do with my family being so poor. My dad was still trying to recover from all his losses.

My favorite memory of this school had to do with Christmastime and the drawing of names for gifts. Nobody wanted by name, so my teacher, Mrs. Allen, took my name. I will always remember her gift, a pocketknife. What a wonderful gift! I had always wanted one of my own. Today, I think about what a big fuss would be made about having a knife at school and how it would never be allowed. But back then it was common and most of the boys had one. We used to play mumble-the-peg, a game played with a knife, at recess. You had to have your own knife in order to play, and now I could play, too! Other than clothing from my parents, this knife was one of the first gifts I ever received.

The only toys I had to play with were a little metal 1947/48 Olds car and a John Deere tractor, both of which my mom had gotten me. I also got a 1946 Chevy truck while I was helping my dad deliver produce in Erie. There is an interesting story about how this little toy truck came into my possession. While helping my dad deliver produce, I saw this little toy truck on the tree lawn in front of one of the houses my dad was delivering to. I picked up the toy truck from the tree lawn and got back into my dad's old pickup. As we got up the street, my dad saw the toy on the floor of the pickup and asked me where it came from. I told him that I found it out next to the street a couple of blocks back and that it looked like someone had thrown it out. I asked if I could have it. He told me that the truck was not mine because no one had given it to me. I had to take it back. He turned around and we back to the house where I had picked up the toy truck. Once we got to the house, I was crying and told him again that it was thrown out so why couldn't I have it? He told me if I wanted the truck that badly I would have to go up to the house and ask for it. If the owner said I could have it, then it was all right with my dad. I jumped out of the pickup, grabbed the toy truck, and ran up to the house. I rang the doorbell and a lady came to the door with a little boy standing beside her. I told them the story of finding the little toy truck on the tree lawn, explained that I did not have many toys, and my dad said if I wanted the toy to ask for it. Boy, was I surprised when the lady said I could have the truck and the little boy agreed. (Keep in mind, this was a well-to-do area of Erie and the little boy probably had lots of other toys.) I have no idea how I ever got up enough nerve to go up to the house and ask for the little toy Chevy truck. I guess I was so young and naïve that I really did not know any better. I learned a few lessons from this experience. I thought that if there was something I wanted, all I had to do was ask for it. Well, let me tell you, that theory was proven wrong the very next time I asked for something and was told no. In fact, this has not worked for me many times in my life. However, I did learn from my dad never to take anything that is not mine. Poor though we were, my dad brought us up to be honest. (P.S. I still have the little red 1946 Chevy truck. It is displayed on a shelf in my family room, and anytime someone asks why I have it, I have to tell the story about the little toy truck. I must have told my son the story a dozen times as he was growing up.)

Anyway, back to the story of the pocketknife. I was getting older now and big boys did not play with cars and trucks. So I was happy to have the knife and now I would be like the rest of the boys and fit in. I did have my own sled and, even though it was second-hand and slightly broken, I was still able to go sledding with the other kids. My brothers did have some big-boy toys that they shared with me occasionally, like their second-hand two-wheel bikes which they would let me ride sometimes. They also had an old BB gun and, under their supervision, my dad would let me shoot it. But basically we had to make up our own fun. With my two brothers I always had something to try and do, though they considered me too young and too much of a pest to be around all the time. I learned so much from them by just watching and following them around. They taught me different things because of their almost opposite personality types. Throughout my life I was to learn from them, especially as I went throught the "Let Richie try it" episodes. I will talk more about my brothers later in the book and give you an idea of what both meant to me.

Alice was closer to my age, but she liked playing with dolls and stuff like that. In school, I was always protective of her and often got into fights because of her. Jr. and Gene were too far ahead of us in school and could not help too much. Sometimes I would go and get them later and tell them what had happened. Gene, especially, would then come and straighten out things pretty fast. He was always ready to fight. Jr. was a little more passive and would try to settle things just by talking. Let me say this, though: Jr. could take care of himself quite well. He was extremely strong as a young man, and my bother Gene was no slouch either. Both grew up to be big, strong men. Gene was 6'5" and weighed 225-250 pounds. Jr. was not as big as Gene, but he was stronger. More later.

CHAPTER 7

Moving Again

We were moving again and, yet again, another new school and low man on the totem pole. This time it was a big move, though, to another state—Ohio! It was a place called Conneaut and dad bought a little farm there. The place certainly needed a lot of work and, again, there was no running water or bathroom. We were back to an outhouse again, but I was used to this by now. As I think back on all these moves we made and doing without what most people considered necessities, I wonder how my mother put up with so much deprivation. It was bad enough for us kids, but she had to cook and clean with no modern conveniences. Of course, we had no furnace either and had to use the old potbellied stove in the front room and the old woodburning stove in the kitchen. That meant tremendous amounts of wood cutting, and one of my jobs was to stack the wood outside the house and in the woodshed, where we kept at least a month's worth. Then I had to bring into the house what we would use for that day. We did not the use the wood only for ourselves, but we sold it to other people, mostly in the city. We did not have the woodshed when we first moved in but, when we built the garage onto the house, we added the woodshed with it. This gave my dad room for the car or truck when either needed to be worked on. I am pretty sure this was the first garage by dad ever had, and it was connected to the house along with the connecting shed. This allowed us to store a large amount of wood without going outside all the time in the winter. We could also access the basement without going outside since the entrance to the basement was also enclosed. Boy, what conveniences we had now!

There were no outbuildings on this farm when my dad bought it. My dad and my brothers built all the buildings that were now a part of this farm. Besides the garage/woodshed which I mentioned before, they built a 30x50 foot barn, granary, corncrib, chicken coop, outhouse, and two additions to the barn. My brothers and I did most of the work, and we were only fourteen, thirteen, and ten in 1952. Things now were taking a turn for the better for the family, and dad had settled up most of his debts. That was why he was able to buy that farm in Conneaut and get a new start. To this day, I cannot imagine my brothers building so much at the farm, considering their ages. Nearly all the buildings are still standing today, over 50 years later! I helped a little but I am very sure it was very little as far as the building was concerned. However, I learned quite a bit from watching and, as I got older, I applied this childhood knowledge of building to help me out in my own life. I would guess that most people would not believe that young boys like us could do most of the work ourselves without much help from our dad. But we did!

My dad obtained most of the lumber we used for building by tearing down a big, old barn across the Ohio/Pa line in Edinboro and moving it to Conneaut.

It took months of hard work and many truck and tractor/wagon loads. We did have some help from a few of my dad's longtime acquaintances, mainly Buck Crosby (where Alice fell off the swing) and John Dorman. Buck helped with the tearing down of the old barn, and John had some carpentry and masonry experience. The place where this old barn once stood is now the site of the clubhouse for a beautiful golf course in Edinboro, PA. The golf course lies on top of a hill on Route 6N while coming into Edinboro from the west. What a beautiful view! It is obvious why a golf course was built there.

While doing all of this, my dad grew some crops and sold the produce. We also started to raise some animals for the farm. By the winter of 1952, nearly everything was in place. We had done a tremendous amount of work in a short amount of time, especially for three boys and a couple of middle-aged men giving some guidance.

I started the sixth grade at Monroe Center Grade School in 1952. It was a little school with all eight grades. Mrs. Wilson was my teacher and she tried her best to straighten me out and teach me something. But I was always acting up and getting into trouble, as usual. To this day, I do not quite know why. I guess I was just trying to get attention and was going about it the wrong way. In spite of my always acting up and giving her a hard time, Mrs. Wilson came to my high school graduation seven years later and congratulated me. She gave me a card with five dollars in it, the <u>only</u> graduation gift I received. I was shocked and elated. Thank you, Mrs. Wilson, wherever you are.

One day that same year some neighbors, Robert and Mary Golden, came down to introduce themselves and visit. This visit brought about a major turning point in Alice's and my life. The Goldens invited our whole family to visit their church some Sunday. My parents turned the offer down for themselves but said that the kids would love to go. Jr. and Gene hurriedly declined, but mom and dad said that Alice and I would love to go. They gave us no choice in the matter and, when we asked why Gene and Jr. did not have to go, we were told that they were older and did not need church as badly as Alice and I did. I guess we acted up more, and I was a little miffed about that. However, my parents thought church would be good for Alice and me, so it was decided that the Goldens would pick us up the next Sunday. Going to church with Mr. and Mrs. Golden that first Sunday set a precedent for Alice and me, which would be repeated for most of the next five years or more. Sometimes my dad would go to church and take us with him, but most of the time the Goldens picked us up.

Alice and I enjoyed going to church. We even got up in front of the congregation and sang songs and recited poems. It was in 1953 that I went forward and accepted Jesus Christ as my Saviour. I did not have a Bible when I first started going to church. The only one we had in our house was the family Bible, and it was real big and we were not allowed to take it with us to church. But on May 3, 1953, I was presented with my first and very own Bible after having learned

44

scores of Bible verses and having perfect attendance. My Bible was presented to me by my Sunday School teacher, Mrs. Alice Eccleston. She taught me not only things of the Bible but of life in general. I have now been saved for over 50 years, and I still have that Bible I received over 50 years ago! The print in that little Bible is hard for me to read now, and I use a large print one now. But that 50-year old Bible is still out for display, mostly as a reminder to me about where I came from. A big thank you to Mrs. Eccleston for all she did for me and for that first Bible.

I also wish to thank the Goldens for being instrumental in getting us started to church. I have kept in touch with the Golden family a little over the years. Mary Golden has now passed away, and Robert still lives at the same place out in the country. He has to be somewhere in his 80's now.

The little church I attended while I lived in Conneaut for about 5 years was the Wesleyan Methodist Church. Going to church there played a significant role in shaping my entire life. I would strongly recommend that everyone go to church and accept the Lord as Saviour. I am convinced that it is important to start children in church as soon as possible. The younger the better. My church experience of learning Bible verses and singing the old-time hymns has served me well in my life and I still benefit from this spiritual grounding even today.

It was hard for me to understand then (and even now) how my dad could drop us off at church but never pick us up when we lived 5 or 6 miles from the church. I guess he thought that one of the neighbors would bring us home. Even though we had neighbor families in the church and many of the children went to school with us, none of them would take us home. I still do not understand it to this day. Alice and I certainly did not knock anyone off, rob any banks, or do anything horrible. But, for some reason, we ended up walking the whole 5 or 6 miles home. Boy, we really did some strange things for only being 10 and 12 years old.

We attended the two-week Vacation Bible School at the church every summer. We had so much fun because we met other kids from surrounding communities. We also made some creative crafts. One summer we made some bookends with a cross on them, and I still have mine. I do not remember too many of the new kids I met, but I do remember a little girl named Judy. She came to our class even though she was from Albion, Pennsylvania, just a few miles away across the state line. I was not interested in girls at that time, but I remembered her for reasons I will later explain.

It was now the fall of 1953, and I was in the seventh grade. I certainly was in for a big surprise the first day of school. I had my first male teacher and his name was Mr. Harry Fernandez. As usual, I was talking while class was going on and, all of a sudden, this book came flying across the room at me out of nowhere! Crash! Against the desk it went. It scared the dickens out of me. Of course, I had to make a scene and mouth off to the teacher and say, "What in the heck did you do that for?" It did not take long for him to come to my desk and grab hold of me and growl, "Mook, I'm not going to put up with your nonsense this year. If you want to be part of this class, you are going to shut up and pay attention. You are not going to get away with your shenanigans in my class. You may have gotten away with this silliness for 6 years but not this year! Not as long as I am your teacher." He said all of this right in front of the class where everyone heard him. I do not know how he knew so much about me. He continued, "You've fooled around now for 6 years. The buck stops here this year, Mook! I see you have a high IQ and yet you have barely passed each year. I don't know why someone hasn't straightened you out before, but you won't get away with it this year in my class. These poor grades have got to go. You have to stop messing around and get your act together." Boy, he sure did chew me out. I was a little embarrassed and had no smart retort when he asked if I had understood what he said. I just meekly replied, "Yes, sir."

Needless to say, Mr. Fernandez made a huge difference in my life. He took an interest in me and even invited me to his house a few times. He taught me some Spanish, even though we did not have that for a class in seventh grade. My grades shot up that year, and I enjoyed going to school for the first time since preschool/kindergarten in the one-room schoolhouse at Woodcock. A big thanks to Mr. Fernandez for all his help, encouragement, and patience with me. I have kept in touch with him intermittently over the years. He is retired now, of course, and is somewhere in his 80's and lives near Rome, Ohio.

Many more changes occurred in the eighth grade. I had another male teacher, Mr. H. Wayne Umholtz. For the first time in school, I received much of the right kind of attention. Mr. Umholtz actually liked me. I had always thought that I would have to act up and fool around to get attention and have someone like me. Boy, I sure was wrong. I got more attention than I had in the previous seven years put together. The school started a basketball team in the eighth grade and, even though I had always been interested in sports, for the first time I was on a competitive and organized school team. (Yes, believe it or not, I made the team.) We only had about 20 boys in the seventh and eighth grades to choose from, but we had a couple of pretty good athletes on the team. It was our first year of being a team so we were too new and not organized enough to win many games. I still had fun playing on that team, though. It was a good start for me in my career of playing sports, and I learned a lot that year from playing on a basketball team. In addition, we used to play baseball at break times. We had a couple of good baseball players who would excel later in high school. Mr. Fernandez and Mr. Umholtz both showed us good plays in football, too, as we played at recess.

Even though school was going so much better and my grades were skyrocketing, I still was having trouble with some of the kids. My clothing and my haircuts were pretty ragtag, so the kids still teased me and made fun of me. My dad or my brothers gave me my haircuts and, let me tell you, they were pretty awful. The kids at school used to really make fun of my haircuts. Even though Gene and Jr. cut each other's hair and they cut mine, I never got a turn to cut theirs. I never understood why I did not get my turn at haircutting. I just let my hair grow instead of putting up with their amateur haircutting skills. Even though my dad was doing better than before, he was still struggling to make a living from the farm and there was no money to go to the barbershop. When I complained about my haircuts, my dad would say, "When you can pay for them, you can go to any barbershop you want."

Mr. Umholtz unwittingly was the cause of much encouragement for me at this time. In front of the whole class, he told me how disappointed he was in my grades. Mind you, I was getting all A's and B's at this time. But this was not good enough for him. He told me that he would not be satisfied until I made all A's. What a compliment that was, backwards though it seemed at the time. For the first time in my life, teachers were actually expecting superior work from me. It did not hurt my image either that he told me all of this in front of the whole class. Now the kids knew that I was smart, at least, even though my clothes and hair did not always look the best. Mr. Umholtz's public praise of me did wonders for me socially.

My dad continued to do better and better on the farm, though he struggled financially as always. He sold lots of produce and even some veal, milk, butter, and eggs from the animals we were raising. He made a living for us and that is about the most that could be expected from that small farm. The biggest sales in the summer were sweet corn, strawberries, tomatoes, and sundry other homegrown produce. In the fall and winter we sold lots of potatoes and apples, along with some oranges and grapefruits from my grandfather's place in Florida. We got most of our potatoes from Shellito's potato farms in Andover, Ohio. When we were growing up, all of us kids and our dad worked every fall at the potato farms there. What a help this was to me because I was able to earn some money to buy some "nicer" clothes for school. I would be going to the high school the next year (1955), so I wanted to look halfway decent and get a better start for high school. Working on the potato farm was a great learning experience for me. It was hard work, but it taught me a good work ethic. I now could understand that if you wanted something, you had to work for it. One of my dad's favorite sayings was: "There isn't always free soup at the end of the line." Now I knew for myself what he meant. I worked part-time for Shellito's potato farms for 6 or 7 years. This is where I got most of my spending money. I also worked for other farmers in the area, doing a variety of jobs. I even started raising some cattle of my own. My first calf came from our old family cow we called Lady. I called my calf Rosie. We named most of our animals on the farm. At one time on this farm, between the boys and our dad, we had 20 head of cattle, the most cattle that we ever had. All of us boys were still in school, too.

In the fall of 1955 I was a freshman in high school. Rowe High School, located in East Conneaut, was so big compared to everywhere I had been before. There was a bigger high school in the city of Conneaut

50

itself, and we had a choice of attending either high school. The country kids and those living in East Conneaut went to Rowe, and the Conneaut kids went to the city school. My brother, Jr., had graduated that spring in 1955. Gene was a senior, and Alice was still in grade school at Monroe Center.

High school was certainly a change for me with many new kids to get to know. One of the first new kids I got to know was a boy named Harry Fails. He was really into sports, especially baseball, and we used to talk sports all the time. He was very popular in school and knew nearly everyone. This helped me out because I would pal around with him, thus getting to know most of the kids pretty well. I did not make any of the sports teams my freshman year, and it was hard fitting in. I concentrated mostly on my grades. Both of my brothers were more athletically inclined than I was but, because of all the work to be done of the farm, they did not get much of a chance to play. However, I was able to stay after school and I went out for all the sports. My brother, Gene, did not think that I stood a chance of making any of the teams, but I kept on practicing and trying. I got to know the coaches pretty well, and they seemed to like me. Both of these coaches, Mr. Stan Humphrey and Mr. Ben Klepek, were to play an important and intrinsic part in my life. In the next three years, I lettered in every sport after playing basketball, football, basketball, and running track. I ran the half-mile and the mile in track and held the fastest time in the mile until well after I had graduated. Our football team did not start up until I was a junior, and I played any position that the coach would put me in, mostly defensive end. We had pretty good teams for just starting out. We had mostly big, strong farm boys on the team, and we did surprisingly well. We were first or second in the county in all the sports we participated in. I liked baseball the best, but it was my worst sport as far as talent was concerned. We had some terrific athletes in our school, even though it was small. I did pretty well at basketball, but again, it was hard to crack the starting lineup. Coach Humphrey had started the same five kids since the $7^{th}/8^{th}$ grades. I was one of the very few from my Monroe grade school to play on the basketball team. In the years I played, I only started one game. In that game, I was second in scoring for the team and I only got to play half of the game. I desperately wanted to play the whole game and asked Coach Humphrey if I could. He said he wanted to give some of the other players on the team a chance to play, too. We were winning the game 50 to 20, and he said there would be other chances for me. I never started another game, but I got to play in many games as the years went by.

The highlight of my high school baseball career was a game in which my friend, Harry Fails, was pitching. Coach Humphrey put me in to play in the 9th inning. I made a good running catch for the last out to save the ballgame. My team carried me off the field! That was a tremendous thrill for me. I loved playing all sports, even though I was not the most gifted athlete. I put forth tons of effort, though, and always played the hardest and best that I could. However, the most difficult part of playing sports was 6 or 7 mile walk home after practices and games. My dad was not too keen on taking me or picking me up, and my brothers were too busy. We lived out in the country, so I had to walk 6 or 7 miles from school every day, regardless of the weather, and my games and practices only increased the times I walked this long distance. I walked those long, dreary miles hundreds of times, rain or shine.

My dad was never too keen on us playing sports because we had so much work to do on the farm. I guess I took advantage of my brothers by staying after school almost every day and not going home to do my farm chores. I still had to do my chores in the mornings, getting up around 5:00 A.M. Even though I got out of some of the evening chores, there was still no free ride at our house and I had to do my share of the work. We were busiest in the summers, with all the fruits and vegetables to tend and harvest, and I worked extra hard then. It sure was work growing up on a farm, but it was an interesting way of life. We struggled more than most, but I learned much about life and have been able to use this knowledge throughout my life.

RICHARD L. MOOK

CHAPTER 8

Bad News for Me

It was now the spring of 1958 and my junior year in high school. I was making good grades and participating in all the sports. I was getting along with nearly all the kids at school, and the teachers all liked me. To be quite honest, things had never been so good for me at school. Jr. and Gene have graduated, and Alice was in the ninth grade at Rowe with me. What could go wrong for me now? Plenty could, because my dad informed me that we were moving back to Edinboro, Pennsylvania. He had sold the farm in Conneaut and we would have to be moved by April 1. I was dumbfounded because it seemed that this was the best my parents had ever done. My dad owned his own place, had cattle, and had a thriving produce business. I honestly do not know why they made a decision to move again. It was not for me to decide, though. With a sinking heart, I told my parents how much I liked the school, teachers, and kids in Conneaut. I explained how well I was doing there in school, both academically and in sports. I did not want to be the new kid again at another school. I desperately tried to explain how I would have a hard time making any of the sports teams for a new school and how important to me it was to make the National Honor Society. These things would be impossible at a new school. All of my pleading seemed to fall on deaf

54

ears. I could be extremely stubborn at times, and this was one of those times. I absolutely refused to go with them. I had not thought it through, but in my heart I knew that I could not give up everything that I had worked so hard for. With no idea or plan about how to accomplish it, I just felt that I had to stay in Conneaut and graduate from Rowe High School.

THE TRAILER — 1957

My dad must have known some of my anguish because he came up with a pretty good idea. He would leave a little house trailer that he owned on the property that we were leaving, after first agreeing on a monthly payment with the new owners. The plan was that I would live in the trailer but would have to pay the monthly rent of $20.00. My dad made me aware that I would have to pay this amount myself and the upkeep on the trailer was my responsibility. The little trailer had propane heat, and I plugged an electrical extension cord into the house my dad had just sold. I am sure that my dad did not think I would really stay there alone and that I would move with them after living by myself for a few weeks. I fooled my family, though. I stayed there for two years and finished out my junior and senior years living in that little trailer by myself. My electric was included with the rent, so that helped. How much electric could I use in a little trailer with only two or three light bulbs? I used the propane tank that was with the trailer to heat it. It must have been full because it never ran out. I was only at the trailer to sleep at night, so I did not use much propane to heat it. I had to go to the house next door and get a pail of water every few days. I would shower at school after practicing or playing sports. Then I went to my mom and dad's in Edinboro every weekend, got some clean clothes, and brought back food for the week. My mother made up food for me that was easy to cook or just heat up. (Too bad there were no microwaves then.) All in all, it was not such a bad situation for me and it certainly was another learning experience.

I loved going to school at Rowe High School and living in Conneaut. Today, I tell people that I was born and raised in Conneaut, even though that is not quite true. I graduated fifth in a class of 60, with a grade point average of 3.8. I was a member of the National Honor Society and received scholarship and citizenship awards. I lettered in all four sports. I have never regretted staying by myself in that little trailer just so I could graduate from Rowe High School. It had nothing to do with not getting along with my parents. It was because I knew that I had found a place where I could excel and I would never have done as well starting all over again in a new school.

Many wonderful things happened at Rowe High School in Conneaut, and I am so thankful I stayed there to graduate. I made some lifelong friends with whom I still correspond today. Many were role models for me and played an important part in my life as I was growing up and even in my adult life. They set examples for me that I instilled in my own life. Let me tell you about some of them.

Harry Fails—Harry was my best friend in school, and we both had a fierce love of sports. Harry was an extremely gifted athlete, lettering in three different sports, and was a class officer in many grades. He graduated from Kent State University and became basketball coach at Conneaut High School in the late 60's. He took the Conneaut basketball team to the state quarterly finals in 1970, the furthest a team from Conneaut had ever gone. Not too bad for a little country school. He then went on to coach at Alliance High School and, eventually, became the athletic director. Harry was there for around 25 years. He is now retired and still resides in Alliance.

Mr. and Mrs. Harry Fails—Even though young Harry was my school friend, his parents were extraordinarily kind to me and treated me as if I were one of their children. On basketball game nights, rather than walk the long distance home after school. I would go to the Fails' house and stay until the game started. Many times they invited me to eat dinner with them. At first I refused because my parents brought us up to not bother other people and put them out, especially by eating with them. However, the Fails family made me feel so comfortable at their house that I ate there several times. I was at their house many other times just to play sports with Harry and, even after high school, I would visit with them quite often. They liked me and trusted me so much that they showed me where they hid their house key, in case I would ever have to come into their home when they were not there. In the winter months there were many times when the weather was very bad that Mr. and Mrs. Fails insisted that I spend the night, so I would not have to walk home in the bad weather. I have remained friends with them throughout the years. They are both still living and are in a nursing home in Conneaut. I have visited with them there, and they remembered much about my school experiences. Mr. Fails had had a stroke, but he was still able to communicate with me very well. I was such close friends with him that he sometimes referred to me as his son. I have exchanged Christmas cards with the Failses for 45 years now, the longest card exchange I have developed over the years. Thank you, Mr. and Mrs. Fails, for all that you have done for me throughout the years and for being my friends. I will always be grateful to you and will always remember your kindness.

Roger Hogle—Roger was a quiet kid in school who set a good example for me in many ways. I am sure that he did not realize that he was doing so at the time. He is now pastor of the Conneaut Baptist Church located on old Route 7. He also played a large role in getting a school started, which is associated with the church. He not only graduated from college but he has a doctoral degree in theology. I do not see or hear from him much now, but I still consider him a friend and big influence on my life.

Richard Nutter—Dick was a good friend in school and was one of the non-sport kids I hung around with. I lost track of him for several years, and we have only recently started up our friendship again. Dick still lives in Conneaut.

Will Clark—Will was another classmate that I got along well with but did not hang out with a lot. He has become a better friend since we graduated from high school. I did not have much contact with him for many years because he went into the military and retired from it after 20 years. Then he went to college after being in the service, got his teaching degree, and taught school for a few years. He now has his own business which he runs with his wife. For the past 20 years or so, Will and his wife host a class breakfast once a year, which about a dozen classmates and I attend. What a nice gesture! Thank you, Mr. and Mrs. Will Clark, for your hospitality.

Judy Nelson Carter—I did not hang out with Judy in high school, although I always got along with her. She has become a friend in the last 10 years because we have a common bond. After I lost my son, she wrote to me and shared with me about losing her son. She was a source of encouragement to me. We do not visit each other, but we see each other at the school reunions and breakfasts. We exchange e-mails a few times a week.

I got along with nearly all of the kids in my class and in the entire school. I was voted the Citizenship Award by my fellow students. This award had to do with setting a good example and getting along with everybody. Being a good student academically and helping others were also considerations for this award. There were many kids in my class who were a big help to me and set good examples for me. I still keep in touch with some of my fellow students and have attended all of the high school reunions. There are many more classmates whom I could talk about and describe, and I would like to say thanks to all my classmates for their various contributions to my life. In addition to my fellow students, there were many teachers who helped shape my life. I will tell you about some of them.

Mr. Howard Hopper—Mr. Hopper was my industrial arts teacher, mechanical drawing teacher, and my freshman homeroom teacher. A good teacher and personal friend of mine, he taught me many skills that I used in my job and everyday life. When I eventually went on to take classes at Lakeland Community College, I took courses in mechanical drawing with the intent of becoming a draftsman. I did not become a draftsman, but I did become a millwright (A class). Mr. Hopper's training helped me in pursuing my lifetime work endeavors. He and his wife attended my wedding, and we remained friends until he died. Mrs. Hopper has passed away, too, but I still keep in touch with their daughter, Susan, who is in a nursing home near Conneaut. She has multiple sclerosis and is confined to a wheelchair. The Hoppers also had a son, who was killed in an automobile accident while in college. I was still in high school then and often wondered how the Hoppers coped with losing their son and taking care of their invalid daughter. Mr. Hopper never talked about his son much but he had his picture displayed prominently in his living room, which I would see whenever I visited him over the years. He certainly did set a fine example for me and played an important part in my life. Mr. Hopper thought so well of me that, when I got my job at Lincoln Electric, he wrote such a glowing recommendation letter that my interviewers almost did not believe one person could have that many good qualities. It almost kept me from getting hired there. (Ha, Ha)

Mr. Stan Humphrey—Mr. Humphrey was my shop (industrial arts) teacher and my coach in all four sports. He liked to talk baseball with me. He was not only my teacher and mentor, but my friend, too. Mr. Humphrey expected the absolute best grades from me, not only in his class but in all my classes. I remember one time we had an essay to write for English class, and many of the kids did not do well on it. In front of the basketball team, he asked how everyone did and most kids received a C or D. He did not say much to them, but when he asked me how I did and I told him I received a B, he was not happy about it. He told me if I wanted to keep on playing basketball, I had better not get a grade like that again. He would not settle for any less than an A from me. Now that I think about it today, that was a nice compliment. Mr. Humphrey went on to teach and coach at Conneaut High School after Rowe consolidated with them. He has since retired and still resides in Conneaut.

Mr. Ben Klepek: Mr. Klepek was my football and track coach. He was not my teacher in any subject, but I got along with him very well and he became a personal friend. We used to talk sports all the time. What a day it was when Mr. Klepek and Mr. Humphrey took me to my first major league baseball game! It was between the Cleveland Indians and the Detroit Tigers. Detroit was my favorite team. I was simply elated over going to the game. I was a junior in high school at that time. My dad never took me to a ball game, mostly because he could not afford it and he did not have the time. He had to concentrate on making a living and did not do much for relaxation and fun. I will always remember those two terrific men taking me to my first ball game. It meant so much to me and I will never forget that kind act. Over the years, I took Richie and his friends to quite a few ball games, and every time I always thought of those two kind men taking me to my first game. Mr. Klepek left Conneaut and assumed administrative positions at Mentor and Willoughby/Eastlake high schools for a number of years. I would often see him at various sporting events and, sometimes, just around town in Mentor, where we both resided. Mr. Klepek passed away of a heart attack when he was only somewhere in his 50's. I went to the calling hours both nights. He was a good friend and an inspiration to me.

Miss Margaret Tobin—Miss Tobin was an excellent math teacher who helped me tremendously. Math was my favorite subject and I excelled in it, partly due to her superb teaching. In my senior year, I placed second in my district in Algebra II and represented Rowe High School at Hiram College in the scholarship test. Miss Tobin always answered my questions and was always willing to help me prepare for this test. She was very instrumental in my achieving this award in Algebra.

Mrs. Evelyn Lynch—Mrs. Lynch, another no-nonsense teacher, taught English. She would only settle for the best from me. Although I always thought she was too hard on me, I can see now that she had only my best interests at heart.

I was fortunate enough to have had all good teachers in high school. I could talk about and praise nearly all of them because they helped me achieve a wonderful education. I will always be thankful to them and for all they did in teaching and preparing me for life. My senior year, especially, was good for me, as I was inducted into the National Honor Society and received the scholastic and citizenship awards. I had fun in the senior class play, playing the part of a policeman in the play called "Father Knows Best." We had our sports banquets and I even attended the prom. In my opinion, the high school years can be some of the best in your life. Contrary to what most might think, the four years went by very swiftly, and I really did enjoy this time.

On May 27, 1959, I graduated from high school. What a happy time that was for me, but it was also a little sad. For the first time in my life, I had felt wanted and accepted. I got along with nearly all of the kids and exceedingly well with my teachers. I still did not have as much as most of the kids, as far as clothes, nice shoes, and things I needed to play sports. However, I sort of fit in with everyone and I was no longer low man on the totem pole. That was a good feeling for me, because I had been down for so long and had so much trouble in grade school.

Today, as I think over some of the problems I had, I believe that much of it was due to the fact of my mother passing away when I was so young and, with my dad struggling so hard, he was not able to give me the attention I needed. So I just acted up and tried to get attention any way I could. I thank the Lord today that He did not allow me to get into any serious trouble. I thank Him for watching over me all those tough years growing up. Attending six schools in the same number of years did not make my life any easier. Of course, the turning point in all this was moving to Conneaut and starting sixth grade at Monroe Center. We all graduated from high school, thus fulfilling my mother's dying request to my father. He did exactly as she asked, and all of us graduated and stayed together. Thank you, dad, and a big thanks to my second mom for all she did to make that wish come true.

GRADUATION 1959

CHAPTER 9

The Real World

It was June of 1959 and I had graduated from high school, ready to face the world. I did not even consider going to college because my family had no money to send me and I needed to take care of myself financially. I had done quite well academically in school but there was just no way I could swing it. Edinboro State Teachers College was close by but, of course, that was out of the question for me. To this day, one of my biggest regrets is that I did not go to college. At that time, there were few loans or scholarships available and I had no one knowledgeable about such things to help and encourage me. Excuses aside, I should have somehow worked things out so that I could have gone to college for at least a year or so. I could always have finished later. However, it was not to be, so I applied for different jobs at some of the factories between Ashtabula and Erie but since I was only 17 years old, no one would hire me. The only place I could get work was at the Shellito potato farms where I had worked off and on for several years. I worked there for $1.00 an hour until I turned 18 and then started applying for jobs in the area factories again. In the meantime I sold produce like my dad did to keep myself in spending money and to keep my old car up and running. I sold a lot of apples that winter.

Jr. had gotten a job at Andover Industries in Andover, Ohio, and I hoped to get a job there, too. The company wanted to wait and see what kind of employee Jr. was before they would consider hiring me. I knew that he would do very well because he was a hard worker and that I would only have to wait a little while before I would be hired, too. I was hired in April of 1960 and eventually moved to Andover. I stayed at the Andover Hotel and shared a room with my brother and another guy named Carl. It was a three-room suite so there was plenty of room for all of us.

Jr. met a special girl, Mary Jayne, there at Andover Industries. After dating for a while, they were married in 1960. They were not married long before he was inducted into the United States Army. Jr. completed his basic training at Fort Knox, Kentucky, and then was sent to Korea for a year or so. I missed him staying with me at the hotel and soon after he left, Carl was taken to jail for some offense. That left me all by myself at the hotel. I was thankful the hotel manager did not raise my rent, and I had the place all to myself. I stayed there for another year.

During the time I worked at the potato farm, my sister would bring her friend Judy with her to pick potatoes. We got a chance to talk and get to know each other a little bit. I found out that she was the same little girl who had come to vacation Bible school when I was 10-12 years old. I noticed that she was not a little girl anymore. She was in the eleventh grade with Alice. I was somewhat shy so I did not pursue getting to know her better or dating her at that time. A year later Alice began dating a guy named Lloyd who was in the Navy and had gone to school with her. He came home on leave with a friend of his, Lefty, and they set up a double date with Alice and Judy. They all went out for a hamburger and shake, but Lefty did not even pay for Judy's meal. She had planned to go out with him on another date the next day, but now she refused. Since my dad was quite strict and protective of Alice, he would not allow her to single date. She decided to fix Judy up with me. After that first date we went out quite a few more times her senior year and I took her to the prom. I thought Judy was the right girl for me, so we were married right after her high school graduation when she was only 17 years old. Graduated one week and married the next! I consider Judy my high school sweetheart, even though we did not go to the same high school or live in the same city or even the same state.

We had a small wedding, mostly family. Judy came from a large family of 13 and there were 4 in mine. We also had some family friends and a few of my high school teachers came. My high school friend, Harry Fails, was my best man and Judy's maid of honor was my sister Alice. We did not have the money to put on a big wedding, but everyone helped out. Judy's mother made a nice four-tiered cake for us and her sister, Marge, provided the flowers for us from the greenhouse they owned. Her stepfather paid for her wedding gown, and her mother made a beautiful veil to go with it. We were married in the East Springfield Federated Church in Pennsylvania. Pastor Farver, the father of one of Judy's school friends, married us. A classmate of Judy's played "Here Comes the Bride" for us on the organ. For the reception held at the home of Judy's sister, Dorothy, everyone who came brought something. With everyone pitching in, the wedding and reception turned out very well. We were pleased. Even the presents were well thought out, with everyone getting together to make sure we had everything we would need to set up a house. There were no duplicates. We spent the night at the place we had rented nearby, and then we left the next morning for our honeymoon in Niagara Falls. I remember as we left that I had to get gas for the car so we stopped at a local station. We still had the "Just Married" sign on the back of the car, and the attendant noticed it and offered his congratulations. When I went in to pay him the $5.00 or so it took to fill the tank, he refused to accept payment and said, "No charge. It's on me." Boy, was I ever surprised. I had bought gas there many times but I did not know this guy very well. That was a big help and a nice present. We had a short honeymoon in Niagara Falls, only for the weekend, and then it was back to work for me on Monday morning.

The house we rented for our marriage was small and had been a tenant house for the hired hand at a farm. The lady who owned the house and farm was Mrs. Grace Weaver, who was a widow with family in the area. The house did not have a bathroom or running water, but it had a pitcher-style water pump at the sink. I honestly do not know how we got by without some basic necessities. We had some used furniture and Judy was able to fix the house up pretty well. I was working at Andover Industries in Ohio, which was a pretty long drive for me in my old junker of a car. In the winter, it was even worse. I sometimes got a ride with one of the foremen who lived in Erie. He had a new Pontiac, so it was a big help when I did not have to drive. However, the $5.00 a week I paid him took a big chunk out of my $60.00 paycheck. It was worth it not to have to worry about getting to work. Thank you, John, for the ride.

Our son, Richie, was born in that little house just before Christmas. We called him our special Christmas present that year. We already had the tree up and the first picture we took of him was under the festively decorated Christmas tree. Judy was determined to be home for Christmas Day, so she was in the hospital for only 48 hours. Judy and Richie both came home on Christmas Eve. I certainly do not know how we made it that first year, with no conveniences of a home and with a new little baby. Through God's grace, we did. Being so far from work and the old car were the reasons we soon decided to move closer to Andover in the summer of 1962.

CHAPTER 10

The Worst Winter of My Life

In the summer of 1962 we moved to Williamsfield, Ohio. We rented a big old farmhouse on top of a hill and it sat way back off the road. It was much closer to my work at Andover Industries. I had been driving 60-70 miles a day and driving an old, unreliable car, so it seemed like a good move for us. The house had a nice setting, especially for the summer and fall, and we had a big yard to take care of. Richie was still a baby and was not big enough to play outside yet, but we still maintained the yard pretty well. Judy was expecting our second child in November. With working at my job every day and keeping up the yard, the summer and fall passed fairly quickly.

The snow started falling early that winter, and I had to shovel nearly every day. The snow just would not stop. Heavy snowfall was an everyday occurrence. It was all I could do to shovel a path just to get my car off the busy road. Every day the snowplow would go by and plow the snow from the road in behind my car. I would have to shovel to get my car out to go to work and then have to shovel again to get back in at night after work. I would usually buy some groceries after work and then have to carry them up to the house. The house was off the road at least a half mile, so I would wade through the snow to get back and forth to the house. It required a lot of shoveling and I could barely keep up with the 30-foot long driveway. With snowing every day and the snowplow blocking my car in every day, it was all I could do to keep up. Judy had to watch Richie and she was close to having the new baby, so she could not help much. I did most of the grocery shopping and took the clothes to the laundromat.

Thanksgiving was getting close and Judy was worried about what we would do for Thanksgiving dinner. The baby was due anytime, and she was unable to cook Thanksgiving dinner for us. I told her I would cook the dinner, but about the best I could do was soup, sandwiches, or hot dogs.

On Saturday, November 24, the snow let up some, and my brother Jr. and his wife Mary Jayne came over to visit and play cards. We used to play Hearts all the time, the boys against the girls. We would play for hours, sometimes until after midnight. They lived nearby and did not have to travel far to get home. In the wee hours of Sunday, Judy left the card game to go into the front room and sit. Mary Jayne went in to see what was happening, and Judy said she was ready to have the baby. Richie had been born in Erie, and we wanted the same doctor for this baby so we had to drive all the way to Erie, 40 miles away. Judy felt that I was too excited to drive and, since Jr. had a much better car than I did, he drove us to the hospital. I have to admit that I was pretty nervous thinking about Judy going into labor and having the baby along the way. I do not know what I would have done. Thank goodness, everything went okay and we made it to the hospital. Jr. had to wait in the visiting area while I went with Judy into the delivery room. A few hours later, our daughter, Deborah Sue, was born. The first words Judy spoke after delivery were, "Now we have a boy and a little girl." She was so happy that we now had one of each. I went down to the waiting area and woke him up to tell him the good news. After a while, we went up and visited with Judy and I showed my daughter to him. A little later we decided to go back to my house and check on things there. I told Mary, Richie, and Mary and Jr.'s kids the good news. Mary said she would watch Richie at her house and I could go back to the hospital to be with Judy. Since I got to name Richie, who was named after me, Judy got to name our new little girl. She named her Deborah Sue because she thought the name was pretty. I brought Judy and Debbie home for Thanksgiving. While the Thanksgiving dinner was nothing special because I prepared it, we were thankful that everyone was fine and we were together. We had a Christmas baby and now a Thanksgiving baby. We had our boy and our girl. We were so full of happiness and were so thankful for our healthy babies. It was a joyous day for us and I thank Jesus for that day.

Christmas was coming, and I did most of the shopping. Judy did not drive and we now had two babies to take out. It was just too cold and there was too much snow to take the chance of getting stuck in the snow with the whole family. We did not have much money to spend on Christmas, but I was able to buy the kids some things and Judy a few presents. I bought Richie some clothes and a couple of little plastic toys. His big gift was a little red wagon, which I still have today. We got that wagon by trading in our S&H green stamps. You would be telling your age if you remember what S&H green stamps were. We would not have been able to afford it otherwise. We also got Debbie some clothes and a little rubber toy squeaky soldier to play with. Her big gift was a doll baby. Judy said she was too little to have a doll, but I insisted and said that every little girl should have a doll baby. I won out, and Debbie got her doll baby. I have both the little toy soldier and the doll to this day. All these toys still hold some precious and sentimental value to me. I bought Judy some clothes, and I particularly remember the red sweater. I took several pictures that Christmas of our little family. I cherish those pictures I took that year.

Christmas and New Year's passed that year, but the snow and cold weather did not. In January of 1963 it was a chore just getting to work. Morning and night, all I did was shovel snow. To make things worse, the water pipes in the house froze up, and I had to get water from the neighbors about a mile away. Going to get the water was not too bad, but carrying it back from the road to the house was a monumental task. I had to carry those milk cans full of water a half-mile up to the house. To tell the truth, I just barely could get my car off the road because of the piles of snow. We lived right off a busy main road, State Route 322, and so the road was plowed frequently. The problem was that the plows kept pushing the snow further and further over to get ready for more snow, and the driveway was hopelessly buried each time. Even if I had gotten someone to plow the driveway for me a few times, it would not have helped. The snow was so relentless that I would have had to have it plowed twice a day, and I definitely could not afford that. The bad winter continued through all of January and February.

On February 23, 1963, it was another cold, snowy Saturday. With so much snow piled in behind my car, I could not get it started for work. A guy who passed by my house for work stopped that morning and asked if I needed a hand. He said I could get a ride to work with him since he was going to Andover, too. Thankfully, I got into his car and told him that I could get a ride home with someone from work. It continued to snow heavily that day and temperatures hovered around zero degrees. At work, I asked a guy who lived in Greenville, PA and drove by my house if I could hitch a ride home with him. He agreed to take me home. Since he worked in the office and finished work at 5:00 P.M., an hour later than I did, I told him that gave me time to stop by the grocery store to pick up some things for the weekend. He promised to meet me at the grocery a little after 5:00. When I finished work, I got a lift to the store and picked up milk, bread, soup, lunch meat, clothes soap, and some other little items. With the weather so bad, I thought I had better pick up enough to hold us over for a few days. I even got meat for Sunday dinner. I figured I had a ride home so I could get a few extra things. I had all my groceries together a little before 5:00 and waited for my ride. The snow was falling and blowing outside, a real winter snowstorm. I was so thankful I had a ride home, but I knew that I had a lot of work to do when I got home, shoveling the snow and getting my car started. I was starting to get a worried when I looked at my watch and saw it was 25 minutes after five. My ride should have been here by now. I really began to worry because I could see how bad the weather was. I decided I would wait a little longer because it would be hard to walk and carry all those groceries. The next time I looked at my watch, it was close to 6:00 P.M. and starting to get dark. In my heart I knew that the guy was not coming, so I did not have any choice but to start the long trek home, carrying groceries with both arms. There were no cars on the street anywhere. The weather was horrendous, and everywhere I looked it was deserted out. Everyone had already gone home, so there was no hope for a ride. So, with my two bags of groceries, one in each arm, I started walking south down Route 7 toward home. I had about 6 miles to go to my house, located a mile or two from Route 7 on Route 322, east of Williamsfield Center. I did not get too far when I realized that I could not carry all those groceries, so I started taking things out of the bags and pitching them, the least needed items first. As I went on for another mile, I threw out some more things. Even though I was young and in good shape, those bags were just too heavy to carry. I could not believe there were no cars going by. Absolutely no one was out in this weather but me. It was a good thing I was dressed for the weather, with a big old coat, gloves, and my hat pulled way down over my ears. Even if a car had gone by, I doubt that I would have gotten a ride the way I looked! By the time I had gone 3 or 4 mile, I just ditched all the groceries. Everything except the milk. I could get by without everything else, but the kids needed the milk. Eventually I made it home about 8:00 P.M. Of course, Judy wanted to know what had happened so I told her the whole story. I was glad to be home but was too tired to shovel snow or worry about my car. I figured I could put everything off until the next day which was a Sunday. I got cleaned up and ate the dinner Judy made for me. We fed the kids and got them ready for bed. They were soon sound asleep. By 11:00 P.M. Judy and I were ready to go to bed ourselves, and we checked on the kids. Richie and Debbie slept downstairs in the same room, Richie in his youth bed and Debbie in her little baby bed.

The next morning, February 24, Judy got up first. I was awake and lying there thinking about what all I had to do that day. The most important thing was to shovel the driveway and get my car started. I needed it to get to work on Monday morning. While lying there caught up in plans for the day, I was jolted back to reality by the most blood-curdling scream I ever heard. Knowing that something was terribly wrong, I jumped out of bed and ran down the stairs into the kids' room where Judy was crying and screaming. I asked, "What's wrong? What's wrong?" She finally said, "Debbie's gone! Debbie's gone!" I looked over at the crib and could see Debbie lying there, not moving. I thought she was asleep. I reached down to pick her up and I could feel how cold her body was. With Judy still screaming and Richie now crying, too, Judy went to pick him up and comfort him.

All of this happened in just a few seconds. We did not have a phone, so I could not call emergency or anybody. I had to physically go to the neighbor's a mile away to make the call. I ran back up the stairs to put my pants on, and then it was back down the stairs and out the door. I was so focused on getting help that I did not even put on a coat. I did put on my old work shoes which were next to the outside door. Without even tying them, I ran out the door with just a T-shirt on. I knew that my car would not start and, even if it did, I could not get it out of the driveway with all the snow piled behind it from the snowplow. I ran through the yard to the road. The snow in the yard had been piling up all that severe winter and was two or three feet deep, but that did not stop me from wading through it. I made it to the road and saw a car coming. I thought that at least I could get a ride to the neighbors. Even a small thing like that would help a little at a critical time like this. I raised my hands and waved frantically, but the car just kept on going. I am sure I must have looked like a crazy person out there in the snow in the zero degree weather with only a T-shirt on. It was only a few seconds before another car came by, and this time I became desperate and ran out into the middle of the road to stop the car. I was determined that this car was not going to pass me by. The only way it would get past me was to run me over. I said a little prayer and the car slowed down and finally stopped. The people in the car rolled down their windows and I told them my daughter was not moving and I needed a phone to call a rescue squad right away. I pointed to where the nearest neighbor was and asked for a ride there. They opened the car door without hesitation, and I climbed in and we rode the short distance to the neighbor's driveway. This driveway was a mess, too, with all the snow piled up and the car got stuck in the driveway. I jumped out of the car, ran to the house, and frantically pounded on the door. A lady came to the door and could see that something was terribly wrong even before I told her of the awful situation. She made the phone call for me immediately and I ran back to the car I had hitched a ride in. By that time, they had dug the car out of the snow where it had been stuck and had it headed out of the driveway pointed toward the road. They drove me back to my house, where I leaped out of the car and, without saying anything to them, ran toward my house. (During all of this, I never did get the names of these people and I do not think I even thanked them in all the hurry and mixup. I will never know who these people were, but I wish I had at least thanked them.)

Back at the house, Judy was still crying and holding Richie, who had no idea of the tragedy unfolding. I do think, though, that he could sense that something was terribly wrong, even though he was so young. Waiting for the arrival of the rescue squad was an interminably long wait. I cannot recall how long we waited, but it seemed like hours. They had to come from Andover and, when they got there, they had to park on the road since they could not get up the driveway with my car blocking it and all the snow. They slogged through the snow to the house, carrying their emergency bags and equipment. I let them in and showed them where Debbie was. I thought they would go through some kind of resuscitation process and at least try to revive Debbie, but they only asked a few questions and said that she was gone and there was nothing they could do. They put a blanket around her and picked her up. They told us they were taking her with them and we should stop by later to make funeral arrangements. I could not believe this. I had focused solely on getting help for her, and now to be told that my precious little girl was gone was too much for me. I was not ready for this and could not even think. I thought, "Debbie is gone! What do we do now?" The neighbor lady came over and asked if there was anything she could do. I asked her to call my brother and tell him what had happened. I did not have any idea what to do, and I thought he could help me make some decisions. Even with Judy there, I still felt so alone. I am sure we were both in shock. Her death was attributed to Sudden Infant Death Syndrome (SIDS) which, back then, very little was known about.

Jr. was not at home, but the neighbor left a message for him that we had an emergency situation. We waited and waited for him at the house so he could take me to the funeral home to make the arrangements. He came over as soon as he got home, which was quite a bit later. He did not know what to say to us and could not express to us how badly he felt about what had happened. It was such a terrrible thing to happen, and no one could express how they felt. It was too horrible. Jr. took us to the funeral home, and Judy and I made arrangements to bury our daughter.

We had to contend with many more problems. We had to make a quick decision on where to bury our daughter. We were young and had not settled in a place to establish ourselves, so we had never even considered where we would be buried, much less our child. I had always considered Conneaut my home. Judy's father was buried in East Springfield, PA. My mother was buried in Guys Mills, PA. We finally decided on the East Springfield cemetery.

The next problem was that I did not have enough money for the service. It was only a few hundred dollars at that time, but that was a lot of money for me then. I was terribly embarrassed when I had to ask the funeral director if he could wait for his money until I got my income tax back. The funeral home was reluctant to do so because we were so young and were not established in the community. They finally agreed to wait, and arrangements were finally made. My brother Jr. put in $20.00 for the flowers. That was a big help.

At last we thought everything was all set, but the funeral home contacted us later that day and told us that there was too much snow in the East Springfield cemetery and they would not be able to bury Debbie until the snow was almost off. We could have the service now and then they would place her in the cemetery sometime later. I did not like this idea at all, but it seemed that I did not have much choice. I thought about everything that had gone wrong and why nothing was going right for me. Who could I turn to for help? It was then that I asked the Lord to help me get my daughter buried now and not have to hold her over.

While I was praying, I also asked if He would help me get a better job so I would never have to face such ruinous financial needs again. It was so hard for me not to be able to have the money to take care of my family's needs. I could see that if I did not make some kind of change I would end up with some of the same problems and difficulties my father had. I could see history repeating itself. I wanted something better. I did not need to be a millionaire, but I needed to make a good enough living so I would never be in the same position again as I was that sad day. I was not afraid to work hard. I just needed something a little better. I asked God to watch over my family and not let anything happen to them. One loss was all I could bear. It was not too much later that the funeral home got in touch with me and told me they would be able to bury my daughter the next day in the East Springfield cemetery. God had answered one of my prayers already!

The next day, we buried my sweet little daughter. There was so much snow at the cemetery that the hearse had to park out on the road and the pallbearers had to carry her over a half mile to the spot we had picked for her. I was one of those pallbearers, and the snow was two to three feet deep in places. To make matters worse, I did not have a topcoat or even a pair of boots. I can still remember wading through the heavy snow in my "good" dress shoes.

The irony of all this is what I found out later when I went back to work. The guy at work, who was supposed to give me a ride home that previous Saturday and did not pick me up at the store as planned, had driven a young lady at work home instead. She did not want to drive her car home by herself in the bad weather, so he volunteered to take her home in his car (conveniently forgetting about me waiting for him at the store). Even though he was a married man and she was single, he had the choice of taking me home as promised or taking her home. It is pretty obvious why he decided to taker her home. (I found out later that he had an affair with this girl.) I was so mad that I confronted him. He laughingly replied, "If you had a choice between taking an attractive girl home or some guy, who would you pick?" To this day, I just despise a married man who runs around on his wife. Though in my mind I relate the passing away of my daughter to the guy who did not pick me up that day, I realize that this incident did not have anything to do with her death. I have not seen or heard anything from that man since I left that employment in 1965, but I did hear a few years later that he divorced his wife. I do not know if he ever thinks about that day or not, but I still do all the time. I have never been able to get over it. Somehow I still put a connection between the passing away of my daughter and his not picking me up. Walking home in that snowstorm that evening taught me a valuable lesson: Don't ever put your trust in humans for they usually fail you. Put your trust in the Lord for He will never leave you or forsake you. What a sad commentary on the nature of mankind. Man's inhumanity to mankind will make countless thousands mourn. What a sad lesson this was for me to learn.

CHAPTER 11

More Problems

Because of the horrible memories associated with it, Judy refused to go back to the house. We had to move out on the spot and had no place to go. Jr. suggested that we move into his place until we could find something. He and his family lived in a big old place that was once a store in Espyville, Pennsylvania. He had plenty of room to store my things, so that was what we decided to do. I was concerned about how we were going to move things from the house when we could not even get close to the door because of all the snow. Again, I turned to the Lord for help and, again, He came through for me. When I went to the house to look the situation over, would you believe the driveway was cleared all the way to the house! What a help! I have no idea how I would have moved everything with the snow all around. It was still difficult to move because Judy refused to go back into the house. I had to pack nearly everything myself, but I did get some help from my brothers and sister. I cannot remember too much about moving all those things to Jr.'s house, but we got it all done in one day.

I found out sometime later that a neighbor a few miles away had come and plowed our driveway. The neighbor's place was known as Wagner Farms. I went to the farm later to thank them and ask a few questions, but I could never really find out who plowed the drive. It sure was a big help and I would like to thank the people responsible.

Things were a little tense at my brother's house, with two families trying to live together. With all the turmoil and tension, I had to find another to place for us to live as quickly as possible. I went back to work a week after Debbie's death, and every day after work I would look for a place to move. I looked at many places but, for some reason or other, I would not be able to rent them. It was either too much money for rent, the place was not livable and a piece of junk, or it was too far to travel to work. I was not too fussy, but Judy definitely did not want to move to the lonely country again or be too far away from people. I looked at dozens of places every day after work for a month or so.

I finally found a nice place that I was sure Judy would like. It was only a few miles from town (Andover) and was close to my work. Even though it was in the country, it was still close to people and other conveniences. I just knew Judy would love it. It had a fireplace, 3 bedrooms, and a nice kitchen with a dishwasher. It even had a big 3-4 car garage that I certainly liked. I fooled around with cars and was always working on my old junker. Boy, this would be great! The rent was around $100.00 a month, which was more than we could really afford. I was taking home about $60.00 a week for 40 hours. It surely was a nice place, maybe a little too nice for us, but I felt we deserved it. It was the house of our dreams. I was pretty sure I could get in some overtime (I never turned it down) and maybe find some part-time work

somewhere.   I knew I could get some work at
Shellito's potato farms later on in the fall when the
harvest season occurred.   My mind whirled with
schemes and possibilities to swing the deal for this
house, even before I told Judy about it because I knew
she would love it. I could not wait to tell her about it.

When I got home that night to Jr.'s place, Judy
could see that I was in a pretty good mood since I was
smiling ear to ear. It was probably the first time I had
smiled since Debbie passed away. I felt a little guilty
that I was happy for that little while. I told her about
the place and begged her to go look at it with me. She
was reluctant and said she was tired of looking at
places that either were too far out in the sticks or were
just dumps. I cajoled her and finally convinced her to
go with me to look at it. We drove to the house, pulled
into the driveway, and she could not believe how nice
the place looked from the outside. She even thought I
was playing a joke on her because the place seemed so
wonderful. I told her it was no joke, but when I told
her how much the rent was, the smile went off her face
and she said we could not afford it. I convinced her we
could.

All this happened on Friday.   When we got
back home, I called the owners and told them we
would rent the place. They lived in Youngstown and
would meet us the next morning at 10:00 to finalize the
deal. I realized I had to work since it was Saturday,
and I could not afford to miss because of the overtime.
I needed the money, especially now that we were
going to rent this house. So I made arrangements to
meet them Sunday at noon. I was so thankful our

prayers were going to be answered. I had asked the Lord to find a place for us to live, a place that He would want us in. I was quite confident that, if the Lord wanted us to have the house, we would be able to rent it.

Now that things were going better for us, we were even talking about going to church again. We had not been going to church since we were married over two years ago. We had gotten busy with work and everything and just did not seem to make time or know where we wanted to go. Boy, what excuses! But things were going better now and we were going to be in a nice place, so now would be the time to start going.

We went to the house on Sunday as scheduled. We even got there a little early. As we pulled into the drive, we noticed there were two cars there already. We thought this meant that they were as interested in renting it out as we were in renting it. We got out of the car and introduced ourselves as the people who wanted to rent the house. I was taken aback when they said, "We're sorry, but we have already rented the house to these other people. We did not think you were that interested and you seemed so young. We thought we would be better off renting it to someone older and more established." Absolutely crushed, I did not know what to say. We turned around and got into the car. Judy was crying before we got out of the driveway. I was, too. I was just stunned. I could not believe what had just happened. This was so hard to understand, especially after praying about it and being so sure that this was what the Lord wanted. After all we had been through the last couple of months, and now this.

I soon found out that what I want is not always what the Lord wants. I should have known this from my past Bible teachings. I figured there must be more to this than what it looked like. The Lord must have had a good reason for us not to live there.

It did not take long for me to figure out the reason. I was reading the paper later that week, still trying to find a decent house to rent. There on the front page was a picture of a burning house, with firemen frantically trying to put the blaze out. As I looked closer and read more, I could see that it was the very house we had so desperately wanted to rent only a few days earlier. It did not take long for me to understand why this was not the house the Lord wanted us in. Had we moved into the house on the spot, as we were planning to do, we would have already been in it when it caught fire. The other people who rented it had not moved in yet, so at least no one was hurt. I still think of this incident in my life today. The Lord certainly was looking out for us, even though I could not see it the day we backed out of the driveway to that house and we left devastated. Thank you, Jesus, for watching over us again.

I did not give up looking for a house. The burning house incident only gave me more strength and convinced me that the Lord had something else in mind. My plans were not the same as His, I thought. Only a few days later, a co-worker came up to me and asked if I was still looking for a place to rent. When I said I was, he told me that the place he rented when he

was first married was available. The landlord had
called him and asked if he knew someone looking for a
place to rent. My co-worker remembered me. I went
and looked at the place and, while it was not as nice as
the place that had burned down, it was suitable for us.

The rental was an upstairs unit over the people
who owned it. The landlords were Mr. and Mrs. Harry
Carr, an older couple. Harry had just retired. The
place was small, but we did not require anything very
large. It was clean, and we could move in right away.
The rent was $40.00 a month, so I did not hesitate and
said we would rent it. They asked if I wanted to show
it to my wife, but I told them she was staying with her
sister in PA and it would be too far away for me to
travel to get her. Really, I did not want to take the
chance of missing out of getting the apartment. They
promised they would not rent it until she had a chance
to see it. Remembering the fiasco the last time I
waited, I did not entirely trust them. I planned to show
it to Judy on Saturday, hoping that I would not be
scheduled to work. I phoned her and told her all about
the apartment. I explained that it was an upstairs unit
over the people who owned it and it was in Andover.
To my surprise, she said to rent it and that she did not
need to see it. She did not care what it looked like or
where it was. That was on Thursday. I planned to got
to her sister's on Friday night and we would leave
early Saturday morning to drive up to Andover to look
at it. (Judy had not felt comfortable staying at my
brother's, so she and Richie were now staying with one
of her sisters. I would drive to see them one or twice a

week and then back to my brother's so I could go to work the next morning.)

Judy still insisted on my renting it right now, but I felt confident that Mr. and Mrs. Carr would honor their promise and wait until Saturday. So we waited and stuck to my original plan. Judy just walked up the stairs, opened the door, and said, "We'll take it." My brothers helped us move in that weekend. 139 Hickory Street, I can still remember the address. It was a nice little place, and Judy fixed it up nicely.

Renting this place was a big turning point in my life. The Carrs were extremely kind people and they made us feel very comfortable. They treated Richie like their own grandson. Mr. Carr built him a sandbox, framing it in first and then filling it with sand he bought himself. He thoughtfully placed the sandbox where Judy could see it from our kitchen window and so they could watch Richie from their kitchen window, too. Richie was never left alone to play by himself since he was not even 2 years old yet. He played in the sandbox for hours on end, using his little trucks to move the sand from one end of the box to the other. Mr. Carr used to play with him many times. He became attached to Richie and was always protective of him. He enclosed the stairs that fall so the cold air would not blow on him as we climbed the stairs to the door.

We became quite close to the Carrs and had a warm relationship with them. They said if we wanted to paint or paper in the apartment, they would buy the materials as long as we did the work. We decided to do the living room over, so Mr. Carr said to buy what we wanted and he would reimburse us. We painted and papered the living room, and then had the Carrs up to look at it. They liked it so much that asked if we would be interested in doing some of the rooms in their part of the house. They would pay me for this. I was happy to oblige and asked when I could start. I was excited about doing some part-time work to make a little extra money. Things were still a little tight for us as far as the bills were concerned. I was so excited that I never quoted them a price, but I knew that Mr. Carr would pay me a fair price. I liked the idea that I did not have to travel to the job—just go downstairs and I was at my job site. While I was doing the work, Mr. Carr would ask if I needed a little money for my work yet. I said I would wait until the work was done. When I was finished, they liked the job I had done and thought it was beautiful. I do not know if it turned out beautiful or not, but I did a pretty good job because I wanted to please them for all the help that they had given us. I did take a little long to do the job, though, but they did not seem to mind. Mr. Carr just said they he was not going anywhere and I could work on it as I had time. I worked nearly every day on it and finished in 3 or 4 weeks.

The hard part came when Mr. Carr asked me how much they owed me. I did not keep track of how many hours I worked since I was just glad to earn some extra money to pay the bills. I thought I would charge about $2.00 an hour because that was what I was earning on my "day" job. I just told them to pay whatever they thought it was worth. I was flabbergasted when Mr. Carr asked me if $50.00 would be okay. I just about fainted as he gave me the check. It would sure help pay the bills.

The Carrs were so nice to us that they even had all the utilities turned on in their name. They would just show me the bill, and I would pay it. The bills amounted to the gas, electric, and water. We still did not have a phone. Even when I did pay the utilities and the rent, Mr. Carr would always ask if I had enough money to cover all of them and if I did not, I could pay the rent the next week. Of course, I always managed to pay all my bills on time. Times were different then. Today, so many tenants stiff their landlords and move without paying all that is owed. And to think that the Carrs had all the utilities turned on in their name! I know I could never have done such a thing. I had to struggle sometimes, but, thanks to the Lord, I was always able to pay my bills. The Carrs certainly did treat us well.

Not every day was good at the Carrs, though. In the summer of 1963, I got a call at work from Mr. Carr. I could not imagine what he would call me for. As I answered the phone a little nervously, I knew that it had to be something important. He said that Richie was burnt terribly and that I should come home immediately. I did not live far from work and was just turning the corner of my street when he flagged me down at the doctor's office, located a few houses from where we lived. I jumped out of the car as he told me he decided to take Richie to the doctor's office first and see what should be done. I went inside and the doctor was wrapping his legs and arms and putting salve over other parts of his body. The doctor said that, even though he had some bad burns, he would be okay. He was not in any danger. Richie seemed to stop crying when he saw me, and I picked him up rather gingerly. I carried him home, and everything seemed to be all right. I finally asked Judy what had happened, and she then told me the story.

She had been ironing in the spare room and had left the iron on the board to cool off. She then went about getting dinner ready. Richie was in his walker, but he could get around in it pretty well. He went into the spare room and grabbed the cord from the iron, and it fell on him inside the walker. He could not get it off him and, of course, he started screaming. As soon as she heard the screams, Judy ran and pulled the iron off him. But by then it had already burned his legs and arms pretty badly, and his chest and stomach to a lesser degree. His clothing helped shield him some, so he was not burned as badly on his torso.

During the night after this incident, Richie started crying and would not stop. We tried everything to get him to stop crying. We held him and gave him milk to drink. Judy took his temperature, and it was 104 degrees. We knew something was terribly wrong, so we took him again to the doctor down the street. We had to wake him up since it was 2 or 3 in the morning. When the doctor looked at Richie, he seemed upset and said he must have an infection from the burns. He gave him a shot of something, some medicine, and told us to take him to the hospital. The closest hospital was in Warren, Ohio. We took him to the emergency room there where they checked him out thoroughly. He did not have an infection but had some kind of flu or virus that was going around. There were no rooms available in the hospital due to the severity of the virus or flu, so they just put Richie in a bed in the hallway. We sat out there and watched him all night. His temperature was down by the next afternoon, so we took him home. I stopped at Jr.'s house on the way home and left him a note telling him that Richie was sick and asked if he would help us watch Richie since neither of us had slept for 48 hours. Judy and I were finding it hard to stay awake. Judy went to sleep as soon as we got home, and I stayed up to watch Richie. The doctor had said to watch him closely so his temperature did not creep back up. If it went back up, we would have to take him back to the hospital. We were so scared because we had just lost Debbie and now Richie was so sick! Jr. got home late that night but, as soon as he read the note, he came right over. He told me to get some sleep and he would stay up with Richie. The next thing I knew it was 7 or 8 in the evening, and Jr. was still watching Richie. We took his temperature, and this time it was near normal. I am so thankful that Jr. was such a big help and was always there for me. He helped me out many times. Thank you, Jr., for all your help and all that you did for me.

In September of 1964, I got another call at work from Mr. Carr. More bad news! My father had another heart attack. He was in St. Vincent's Hospital in Erie, Pennsylvania. I went home and told Judy I was going to the hospital to see my dad. He was not doing very well, and I knew it could be the last time I saw him. When I went back outside to get in the car to leave, my car would not start. Mr. Carr saw that I was having trouble with it, so he offered me his car to use for the trip. He had just bought a new car and had only put a few hundred miles on it. I recall that it was one of the little Fords they were making in those days. Since I knew I was in a hurry and would be driving faster than usual, I declined his offer. I did not want to take a chance on damaging his car since it was new and was not even broken in yet. He still insisted I take the car, saying that if something happened to it, they would fix it or just get a new one. It was covered under warranty, and he was not worried. What wonderful people the Carrs were!

I told him that I would drive my old truck, even though it was not in too good of shape. It was an old 1947 Ford pickup. It did not go too fast, but it got me to the hospital to see my dad. My dad had heart problems, but back then they did not have the technology to do bypass surgery. So he ended up suffering from a heart attack. By the time I got to the hospital, he was not doing too well but I still got a chance to talk to him. All of his children and my mom were there with him. He passed away that evening with me by his side. He did not have a will, but his wishes were to be buried with my real mom in Guys Mills, Pennsylvania. That was where he had been born and raised for the first 30 years of his life. All of his family was buried there. Even my great-grandparents were buried there. Alas, this was not meant to be. My second mom wanted him to be buried in the Edinboro cemetery in PA. None of us kids could get her to change her mind. She said that dad had told her that he wanted to be buried in Edinboro. And that was that! My mom was his wife and, without a will, she had the final say. She said that she would be buried there, too. I thought, "At least dad will be with his second wife, so I guess that won't be so bad." There was no use arguing about it anymore. This was a bad time to be arguing about something like this anyway, so we had dad buried in the Edinboro cemetery. Dad did not have any money or insurance policies, so I bought the lot and paid to have the plot opened for his burial. The rest of the expenses would have to wait until his estate was settled and/or we would figure out how to divide the bills among the kids.

It was very hard losing my dad, especially so soon after the loss of my daughter. I sure do miss the "good old days" stories that dad would tell. I miss not having him here to ask questions about the different things that would and will happen in my lifetime. We had a tough life and grew up in some hard times, but he always did the best he could. The most important thing for him was to keep the family together, and he did that.

We had some good times, too. I remember the times we went bowling together. Dad did not really know how to bowl, but he sure did have fun trying. Even if he only knocked down one pin, he thought that was just great. The score did not make a bit of difference to him. My dad did not do too many things for fun. He was always pretty serious, but he did like to dance and enjoyed his trips to Florida to see my grandfather and bring back produce to sell. He pretty much concentrated on raising us children. He did that pretty well, as we are all grown now and married and have children of our own. My dad kept his promise of keeping us all together and having all of us graduate from high school.

My dad was truly a different kind of dad—a dad that, despite our poor background, could be respected by all his children for persevering and finishing his race. (II Timothy 4:7) I love you, Dad. Thanks for all you did for me. Thanks for all you taught me. Sometimes it was hard to understand what you were trying to teach me, but I sure did learn valuable lessons that were to help me throughout my life.

As I was growing up, I did not fully understand the grief you must have gone through after losing your wife (my mother) and baby daughter (my sister). After the loss of my own daughter and wife, I could more readily understand a little more of the trials and grief you must have gone through. Many times when I was down and did not know how to cope, I thought of your example, how you persevered and finished out your life, even though it was very seldom an easy one. I thought, "If my dad could do it, then so can I."

I did not have the same obstacles to overcome as you did, but finishing out my life will not be easy for me, either. I honestly do not know how much you relied on the Lord for help, but it seems He was there watching over you, too. You see, Dad, I not only had your strength to draw on, but I had the Lord's, too. I have lots to be thankful to you for, but I cannot thank you enough here on earth today for your showing me the strength to go on. I will meet up with you again someday to thank you personally.

Dad, since you have been gone, I have lost my son, and you have lost two of your sons. I know that you are together with your sons and, eventually, I will be with mine. We will all be together. Thank you, Dad, for all you did for me.

CHAPTER 12

Time to Move: A New Beginning

It was the spring of 1965. The bills were still coming in, and I was still getting behind on them. Some of this was due to my dad's funeral expenses. Jr. had paid for some of the bills, but Alice and Gene were not in a position to pay for anything. So the responsibility was up to me to pay for at least half. I still had an old junker for a car, and I could not ever see being able to buy a house. I was still depressed over the loss of my daughter and my father. I knew that if I ever wanted to do better for my family I would have to make a move soon.

I thought about my family's future a lot and decided that there were no good, high-paying jobs in the immediate area. "Where could I go?" I wondered. I used to run into a teacher from Andover High School every now and then by the name of Mr. Richard Kirker. I played sports against his son, Richard, when I was in high school. One day I ran into him on the square in Andover and asked him what his son was doing now. He replied that Richard was working in Cleveland, actually in Euclid, at a big factory called The Lincoln Electric Company. He was doing very well there and had bought a house in Mentor. He had a new car and even had a nice boat, all after working there for a little over a year. It all sounded pretty good to me. This must be the place to work. I went home and told Judy all about meeting Mr. Kirker and what he had told me about his son working at Lincoln Electric. We both thought it sounded like a great place to work, and I decided to check it out.

My brother, Jr., had gotten a job at the Chevy plant in Warren, Ohio. He liked it there and was making much better money than he had at Andover Industries. So I put in applications at Lordstown, "the Chevy place," and other places around Warren. I then put in an application at Lincoln Electric and other places around the Cleveland area. I prayed and asked the Lord to help me find a better job, one where I could pay off my bills, get a better car, and buy a house of our own. I told the Lord that I did not need to be a millionaire but just needed a job so I could take better care of my family than I had been. The Lord answered my prayer several times over, and, to my delight, I was called to work at several places all at the same time.

After discussing it with Judy, we decided that I should take the job offered at Lincoln Electric in Euclid. It was very different from my old job. The work was extremely hard, but I had already quit my old job so there was no turning back. I had to give this a chance and make it work. I drove back and forth to Euclid for about two weeks, a round trip of over 100 miles a day. Coupled with the fact that I was working 12 hours a day, this was just too much, so we decided to move to Euclid. We rented an apartment only a mile or so from work. On Friday, after work, my brothers helped me move again. We made the move in one big flatbed truckload. (NOTE: I could not move today with 10 loads in the same size truck.) It took all night to move and somewhere along the way I got some sleep. I had to work the next day. In the morning, when I woke up to get ready for work, my brothers were eating breakfast with Judy. I only had time for a cup of coffee and a big thank you to them for all the help.

The work at Lincoln Electric was hard, and I was ready to quit at least a hundred times that first year. But I had made up my mind to stay at least one year and give it a try. The Lincoln Electric Company was known for paying large bonuses, determined by how much profit was made for the year. The bonus was always paid the first Friday in December. I worked that first year waiting for December to arrive.

My wages during that first year were not all that great. I was not earning much more than I did at my old job, especially considering that the cost of living in Euclid was greater than in Andover. As an example, I paid $40.00 a month for rent in Andover and paid $140.00 in Euclid. The utilities were in ratio to the amount I paid for rent.

December was finally here, and I was getting my first bonus! I had already tried to figure out how much I was going to get and how we were going to spend it. I was so excited when I received that first check and could hardly wait to open it. I decided to wait until I got home to share it with Judy and Richie. My first bonus check was for $2300.00, the most money I had ever seen before at one time. Even though that was a lot of money for me at that time, it was still short of what I figured on getting, so I was a little disappointed. Every year after that, I have never been able to figure out how much my check would be for or even try to figure what the bonus multiplier would be. I learned a valuable lesson about "not counting your chickens before they hatch" from this experience. Oh, I was thankful for what I got but, after all was said and done, it just did not pay all my bills. The biggest bill was for my dad's funeral expenses. I also had plans to get another car, some new furniture, and a few other things, but all that would have to wait. The only thing we did for ourselves was go out for dinner that Friday. That seemed a little anticlimactic after working that hard all year.

The physical part of the work was so hard that first year that I lost 60/70 pounds. I was a little heavy when I started at 225 pounds, but going down to 160 pounds was really skinny for me. Most of the people who knew me thought that I was sick or something was wrong. I started out working in production and then went into the maintenance department after about a year. That was much better. I liked it because I was always learning something. I learned things that even helped me at home as there was always something to do in maintaining a home.

The second year was better, but it was still hard getting used to work at Lincoln. Euclid was a big city to me, and I was a country boy. The second year bonus was better and now, with all the bills paid, we decided to buy a car. We could not afford a new one, but I bought a used 1964 Chevy. It was immeasurably better than the one I had, but it had pretty high mileage. That car was a necessity, so we decided to buy something for ourselves, a luxury. We bought a color television. We probably would not have bought it since we only stopped at the TV place to "look." That was in October or November of 1966. We told the salesman that we would not have any money to buy until December. I explained where I worked and the bonus system. He said that was all right. They would let us take it home and try it for 30 days. If we liked it, we could buy it then. If not, they would pick it up. After 30 days of watching a 25-inch color television instead of our old 19-inch black and white, there was no comparison. Judy would not have let me take it back for anything, so we bought the TV. That took most of our bonus, so I had to work another year to get ahead a little.

One year led to another, and Richie started kindergarten in 1967. One day when he was walking to school, some older kids jumped him and beat him up. He was injured pretty badly. We took him to Richmond Heights General Hospital, and it was there that the doctors discovered he had a ruptured spleen. He had to have it removed, and he was in the hospital for a week or so. When he finally came home from the hospital, he seemed afraid to go outside and just wanted to stay inside all the time. He did not finish kindergarten that year. Richie could identify the kids who had jumped him, but nothing was ever done about it. I pursued it by going to the police and the school board where I told the story over and over, but to no avail. The response was always the same, "Kids will be kids." We decided to make another move.

We had lived in the apartment in Euclid for four years and had not thought about where we would move the next time. I had gone to an auction sale out in Mentor a short time before this, and the lady that owned the house was moving out of town. The place was small, but we could move in right away. We did not look anywhere else. We felt that this was the place. The lady who owned the home was older and seemed like the perfect sweet, little, old lady. She was anything <u>but</u>.

We moved into the house in Mentor, Ohio, in June of 1969 and had trouble from the beginning. I had to do a tremendous amount of work on the place, and the landlady did not want to reimburse me for anything. I did not mind so much doing the work, but I did want to recoup money I put out for materials. Later on that winter, I had a lot of trouble with the furnace and had to have it repaired several times. The most costly expense was putting another blower motor on the furnace. As usual, I was not reimbursed for anything. Then the water pipes froze, and I had to do a lot of repairs there, too. I did the work, but no help paying for the parts was forthcoming. The landlady just kept telling us to send in the rent and she would settle up later. She never did. All the while looking for a place to buy, we put up with all this nonsense until school was out. After all this trouble renting, we had made up our minds that we were going to buy a house this time. If I had to do all the work and pay for the materials, it might as well be on my own home.

We looked at innumerable houses, but this time we decided not to move until we found exactly what we wanted. We finally found a place in Mentor that we both liked and which seemed to meet all our criteria. I had always wanted to build a new house, but that would have to wait. This particular house in Mentor was nice for us and would do for a while. We were getting tired of renting and doing all the work a homeowner would do and not getting anything in return.

We had a problem with getting our money back from the lady we rented from. By this time, she owed us around $300.00. The only way we figured we might get our money back was to withhold the rent for a few months. So that is what we did. It took a couple of months for our loan to go through and, when it did, we were ready.

We moved into our "new house" in Mentor, Ohio, in July of 1970. My brother-in-law, Lloyd, helped me move this time. It did not take too long because we really did not have too much. In fact, the house looked rather empty. We had lived in 2-bedroom apartments for so long that this house seemed huge. It was not really all that big, but, to us, it was gigantic.

Now there was one more obstacle to overcome. The lady whom we had rented from had her lawyer send us a letter stating that we still owed two months back rent and we would have to go to court to resolve it. I got in touch with her lawyer and with the Lake County Housing authorities and, representing myself, went to court. When the judge heard the full account of what had happened from her lawyer and the Lake County Housing people, plus all my bills and my version of why I did not pay the rent, the judge testily told the lady's lawyers that she was lucky that I was not suing them. He said that a house cannot be rented without heat or running water, unless it is fixed immediately. He asked the lady's lawyer what we owed and was told $280.00 for two months rent. He then asked me what I was owed for materials and labor, and I said, "$280.00!" The judge slammed the gavel down and said, "It looks even to me. Case closed!" That was the end of that. I never heard from the lady again.

We certainly did enjoy our new home. Things were going pretty well at work, even though it was tough at times. Richie started school that fall. He was in the first grade and could walk to the school from our house, about a half mile away. We did work around the house, painted, and papered, like most young couples do. Judy planted flowers, and we planted a garden. I had a garage to tinker around in. What more could anyone want? That year went by pretty fast, and the next year we decided to take a nice vacation. We were going to Disney World in Florida. I had just purchased a new 1971 Chevy truck and bought a little camper to go on it. This would be nice for all of us. I had never been to Florida, even though everyone in my family had. They had all gone with my mom and dad when they went to see my grandfather, who lived there. This would be a real treat for all of us. We really enjoyed ourselves, and we stopped and saw lots of things along the way. The "new" Chevy truck made the trip just fine.

We stayed at the same Mentor location for the next eleven years and kept Richie in the same school system. Judy had gone to the same school for all 12 years and, as I said before, I went to 6 schools in the first 6 years and finished out the last 7 years in the same school. There was no doubt in our minds that it was better to stay put. I asked Judy and Richie several times in those 12 years if they wanted to move or not, and they both said they wanted to stay.

I would have liked to move and build a new house, but it was better for Richie to stay in the same school system. Richie was on the high school student council and lettered in 3 sports, either by playing or being a manager on the sport teams. One of his biggest thrills was to start the game for the Mentor High School soccer team in the all-senior game. He was proud beyond reason. All his teammates were happy for him, too. He was always so proud of the big "M" on his letter jacket.

Even though Richie had trouble with his grades in school, he stuck to it and graduated in June of 1981. That was a great day. He was so proud of his diploma, and so were we. We had a party for him later that month with some friends and family.

Even after Richie graduated, Judy still did not want to move. I was doing well at work and had decided to stay and retire from Lincoln Electric. By that time, I had in about 17 years and was close to 40 years of age. I thought it was too late to make a big change now. With all of these considerations, we decided to stay where we were.

CHAPTER 13

1983-84 Not Good Years

In 1983 my second mother passed away. I was called at work and told that my mother was in the hospital and was not doing very well. Up until a year or so before, she had been doing pretty well until she fell and broke her hip. She had the hip operated on and pins were put in it. The hip did not heal right, and she had to have it rebroken. My mom was not happy about this, and it took her quite some time in therapy to be able to walk again. She was never quite the same after that. She seemed to have given up a little, but I was still surprised that she was bad enough to have been taken to the hospital. I stayed with my mother that day and into the evening. I was holding her hand when she passed away.

My second mom, whom I always refer to and recognize as my mom, meant the world to me. She had come to our house as a housekeeper in 1947, a while after my birth mom died. She originally came to help my dad because the State and County authorities were about ready to take us away from our dad. Since my dad had so much trouble finding women to watch us little kids, she stayed and helped my dad and eventually they were married and she became my mom. She had helped raise me since I was five years old. She did a pretty good job raising us kids, especially with the circumstances and conditions she had to work with. Without her coming and helping my dad when he was in such dire straits, our family would never have been able to stay together. Who knows where we would be now? A big thanks and a tribute to the mom who raised me. I can never thank her enough for what she did. Thanks again, Mommy!

Mom became a grandmother to all our children. Like all grandmas, she was good and kind to all of them. I think she might have favored Tiny (Gene's oldest) the most, since he was the first grandchild. She helped raise us and stuck by my dad until he died in 1964. They were married for 17 years. After staying by herself at the farm in Edinboro, Pennsylvania, for a couple of years after my father's death, she decided to move and stay with her daughter in Lake City, Pennsylvania. She resided there until her death in 1983.

As we prepared for mom's funeral, we ran into some problems. My mom had a daughter, Marie, whom she was living with, and a son, Raymond, from a previous marriage. Marie placed the obituary in the paper and my brothers, sister, and myself were listed as stepchildren. I had never thought of mom as anything but my own mother, so I was taken aback when the newspaper described us as stepchildren. It hurt me to the core. I probably could have let that go, but when the funeral director told me that I could not sit in the front row for her funeral, I "saw red." He said the front row was reserved for family and I was not considered to be her son. That was really hard for me to understand. She had always referred to us as her children. My mother did not actually raise Marie, as she was taken away at a young age to a girls' home. I never really understood the circumstances. Mom was with us many more years than she was with her own children. In fact, her son was not even in attendance at her funeral. He had moved away several years before, and nobody had heard from him since.

With all this in mind, I know that what I did the next day was not a very good idea but it seemed like the right thing to do. I certainly did not do it to disrespect my mother. Just the opposite, I did it to respect her and show how much I loved her. I arrived at the funeral home early. As I was the first one there, I sat down in the first row in the first seat. The funeral director said that I had to move because the front row was reserved for family only. My wife, son, brothers, and sister were by that time seated a few rows back. I just stoically sat there as the funeral director patiently explained again that the front row was reserved for immediate family. I just as patiently told him that I was a son and asked him if that was immediate enough. I think he finally got the picture and realized that I was not going anywhere. Rather than cause a scene, he left me alone after that.

The next problem arose when Marie decided that she was going to bury my mother at the Fairview Cemetery with her dad, mother, and some of her brothers and sisters. I spoke up and said that mom wanted to be with my dad in the Edinboro Cemetery. That was not meant to be. Since Marie is the legal daughter of my mother and we were "only" stepchildren, we did not have any say in where she would be buried. Because of all this, my real mom is buried in Guys Mills, my dad in Edinboro, and my second mom in Fairview. Boy, what a mixed-up deal! Now my second mom is not with my dad, nor is my dad with my real mom. My dad had said several times that he wanted to be buried beside my real mom, and my second mom said that she wanted to be with my dad. None of this happened. The moral of this story is: You had better have it in writing. They are all gone now. May they all rest in peace.

It was Monday, the week of Thanksgiving in 1983. I had been working six days a week for a long time, and I was looking forward to having Thanksgiving Day and the rest of the week off. It would be such a treat not having to go back to work until the Monday after Thanksgiving.

On that Wednesday before Thanksgiving, I was running late for work. After parking my car, I had to rush to get punched in on time. I was half running and was about halfway there when the chest pains started. I wondered what this could be and I slowed down to a very slow walk. I very seldom was sick and had never experienced chest pains before. To be honest, I had never ever missed a day's work in my life. I might have had a headache or maybe a touch of flu, but I had never felt like this. I had no idea what might be wrong. I got to the shop entrance doors and started walking down the tunnel. (The tunnel goes under the shop where I worked, and then I had to go upstairs to punch in my timecard.) The tunnel had never seemed this long before. As I got to the end of the tunnel, I just knew that I could go no farther. As much as I wanted to get my timecard punched in upstairs, I just knew that I could not make it. I was lucky to have made it that far. The nurse's station was right there at the entrance to the east/west tunnel. As I walked in, the nurse asked what was wrong. I told her I was having chest pains. She immediately sat me down and checked my heart rate and blood pressure. Everything seemed to be okay, but she told me to lie down and rest for a while. I seemed to be doing all right, but she called my boss upstairs and told him what the problem was and that I would be late punching in.

Lincoln Electric was a difficult place to work. They frowned on their employees being late for work or missing work. An employee was required to call in immediately if there was a problem. After resting for an hour, I thought I was doing all right. The nurse checked me out again and said I could go to work. That day, I took it pretty easy and did not have any more problems until I started to go home. As I was going up the stairs to the front doors to the parking lot, I started to get the chest pains again. I continued to my car at a slow pace and felt okay again. It seemed that I only had the pains when I exerted myself.

When I got home, I told Judy what had happened that day, and she was obviously concerned. I kept insisting that I was all right and really did not feel sick. I went to take a shower and get cleaned up for dinner. I was washing myself when I started having the chest pains again. I was barely able to finish my shower and was exhausted. Judy wanted to call the rescue squad and get me to the hospital. I talked her into just driving me there. I did not really want to go because the next day was Thanksgiving. I figured I had a few days off to rest and that was all I needed.

We went to Euclid General Hospital that Wednesday evening to the emergency room where they checked me out and could not find anything alarming. However, they wanted to admit me for further tests. The doctor came in and scheduled me for a stress test right away. To make a long story short, I did not pass it. I was only on the treadmill for a minute before the doctor stopped it and sent me down for a catheterization test immediately. I did not pass that either and he told me one of my main arteries had 98% blockage. The doctor explained that they wanted to perform angioplasty, a procedure where the surgeons go into the artery and use a balloon to open up the artery. This is now commonly known as the balloon procedure. This procedure was just in its trial stages at this time. He explained that Euclid General did not perform this procedure and I would have to go to the Cleveland Clinic, which is world-renowned for its cardiac center.

The only problem with going to the Cleveland Clinic was that they were all booked up for the procedure. Unless this was an emergency of life-or-death, they told me I would have to wait a few days. Even though we felt apprehensive about the wait, the doctor felt that I would be okay for a day or two. He would send me to the Clinic the first opening they had. In the meantime, I would stay at Euclid General so they could keep a medical eye on me.

By this time, Judy had called my brothers and sister and told them about my problem. The next day was Thanksgiving, and Judy and Richie came to visit me. Later that afternoon, my sister and her husband, Lloyd, and their children came to visit. For some reason I still do not understand, Judy became upset with them being there, and words were exchanged. The timing for this was definitely bad when I was doing so poorly and desperately needed an operation right away. I did not need the extra stress of family feuding. I think that Alice and Lloyd could sense this, so they said good-bye and left. To this day, I still do not understand what the problem was.

I was finally scheduled to go to the Clinic on Monday. They sent me in an ambulance because they did not want to take any chances of something going wrong. They would be responsible if it did, and they wanted to make sure I got to the hospital without having a heart attack first. When I got to the Clinic, it took a while to admit me and to get settled in a room. The next day, they did all sorts of tests and scheduled me for another catheterization, even though Euclid Hospital had sent their results. I guess before the Cleveland Clinic did anything, they wanted to look for themselves and do their own tests. The tests revealed the severe blockage, so they scheduled me for the angioplasty procedure for the next day. So, with Judy and Richie in the waiting room, I had the balloon procedure done. The operation was deemed successful, and I was able to go home within the next few days.

I decided to take vacation time and even some extra time to stay at home and rest. I wanted to make sure everything was okay. I returned to work on

January 2 to my regular job with no restrictions. I tried watching myself the best I could, and everything seemed to be going okay. I was back at work for about 7 weeks when I started having chest pains again. I immediately called Dr. Pamelia, and he had me come to his office to check me out. He gave me another stress test and, again, I failed it within a minute. He sent me to the hospital to have another catheterization test. I failed that, too, and he said the blockage was there again. This meant another trip to the Cleveland Clinic and another catheterization procedure.

I was concerned about why the previous balloon procedure had failed. The doctors explained that the procedure was relatively new and was not perfected yet. He said that in some cases where the plaque was pushed up against the artery walls, it does not stay. The doctors did not want to do bypass surgery on me because I was so young. It was also much more expensive. They decided to do the balloon procedure again.

There was another problem this time by the name of King Hussein of Jordan. He came to the Cleveland Clinic for some tests and, for security reasons, he took out a large portion of the heart patient floor. They had to put me on the floor where there were many cancer patients. It was hard for me to understand how one man could take up so many rooms when there were so many people in need of heart surgeries. They were either postponed or were put onto another floor to wait. What if something had happened to me while I was waiting for King Hussein to move off his floor?

This time in the Clinic, there was security everywhere. No one was allowed on the part of the floor where King Hussein was. Even though I was going to have another angioplasty procedure, I did not have to stay in bed the whole time. I was able to walk everywhere on my floor, and I met lots of people during those few days. Each person I met had a story to tell. All of these wonderful people played a large part in my maintaining a good attitude as I waited for the King to move and as I got ready for another surgery.

My roommate's name was Charlie, and he was an older man from West Virginia. He was in his 70's and had already had one lung removed in an operation a few years before. The cancer had returned, so now he had to have a large portion of the remaining lung removed. It is really hard to believe how much of the lungs can be removed, and people still survive. Charlie was quite optimistic and was looking forward to playing golf that summer. He had his operations, which were successful, and he was able to go home. He wrote to me later that summer and sent me a picture of him with his trophy that he won at a senior golf tournament. Amazing! Thank you, Lord, for watching over him.

I also met a young man who had just had his leg amputated. His girlfriend was visiting him as I stopped by his room to visit. They were supposed to get married that summer. I do not know what happened to them, but seeing so many people with such difficult, physical problems was humbling.

I met a little girl around 8 or 9 who had some form of leukemia. The most striking thing about her was that she never stopped smiling. Her grandpa was always with her, and I would talk to him sometimes. But that little girl did most of the talking, and I would just sit there and listen. I do not understand how she could be so cheerful all the time. She was the most beautiful little girl I had ever seen, except for my daughter. She had this long, blonde hair and rosy cheeks. But the thing I remember most was her smile. Even though this may sound strange, I could just picture my daughter looking just like her. I do not know what happened to her, though I did have the grandfather's address at one time. They lived around Warren, Ohio.

I went to the children's floor and talked to some of the kids. So many little children with so many problems. I even visited the baby floor. Even the wee little ones had lots of problems. The water head babies were the hardest for me see.

The Cleveland Clinic is a big hospital with thousands of patients there every day. It is still hard for me to understand why so many people have serious health problems. It sure did put things in perspective for me. I am extremely thankful that we have such good doctors and wonderful health facilities throughout the world, especially here in the Cleveland area. The Cleveland Clinic is one of the best hospitals in the world, and they are the world's leader in heart-related problems.

I met more people during my stay at the Cleveland Clinic, but the ones I mentioned are the ones

I remembered most. They had a big influence on me and caused me to look at things a little differently. Now when I think about being on that other hospital floor instead of the heart floor, I know it was not a coincidence. I know the Lord wanted me there for a purpose. God bless them all.

King Hussein finally moved out, and I was put on the heart floor. It was strange that I was put into one of the rooms that he had occupied. I even thought that I might get a chance to meet him somehow. I am a ham radio operator and King Hussein (JY1) is, too. I told that to the security guards, but it still did not help me get a chance to meet him. I used to think that I would never be that close to the King again, but, now that I think about it, I will be a lot closer to THE REAL KING someday. Thank you, Jesus, for teaching me some valuable lessons the week I was on that floor waiting for my heart surgery.

Back to the heart floor now where I was getting ready for my operation. I was more nervous this time, especially because they were going to operate on February 24, the date my daughter had passed away. With Judy and Richie in the waiting room, they performed the heart procedure on me for the second time. This time they called it a success. I went home the next day or after. I did not stay at home too long this time and went right back to work at my old job, again with no restrictions.

I was back at work about six weeks when the chest pains started again. I went to the nurse's station again, she checked me out, and said everything seemed to be okay. I asked her to call my doctor, and I heard her say she thought it was just in my head and she did not think anything was wrong. As I went back to where she was talking on the phone, I could hear Dr. Pamelia say to her rather loudly, "If Richard says there is something wrong, there is! Send him to my office right away." I left work and went to his office which is a mile or so from work. He looked me over and gave me another stress test. I failed the test again. He told me he would not do another catheterization, but would call ahead and refer me to the Cleveland Clinic again.

I was now in the hospital for the fifth time in five months. As the doctors checked me over, they found that the blockage had come back. They decided they would do a bypass operation this time. This would be more serious than the procedures I had gone through before. It was April 10, 1984. There were quite a few surgeries scheduled ahead of me, and they still had a lot more testing to do. Bypass operations were not routine and were not done unless it was a matter of life or death. They found out that my potassium was low, and they had to get this up. I had to have many more X-rays and go through a series of breathing exercises. They finally scheduled me for April 13 in the afternoon. The doctors decided to lower my heart rate so my heart would not have to work so hard. That evening just before my doctor went home, he gave these specific instructions: "If Richard's heartbeat goes below 40 beats per minute, call me, regardless of the time. Otherwise, the operation will go on as scheduled."

I was pretty nervous that night. Judy and Richie came in to visit me, as usual, and left about 8:00

P.M. They said their goodbyes and promised to see me the next afternoon before the surgery. Before they left, they also promised to call my brothers and sister to let them know the schedule. Later that evening, when the nurses saw that I was still not asleep, they asked if I needed a sleeping pill or a Valium to relax me. I was rather anxious and was not sleeping, but I have this funny thing about not taking any medicine, especially ones that I refer to as drugs. I had never in my life taken anything more than aspirin, and I don't even like to take many of those. So I told the nurse that I did not need anything and would be able to go to sleep. I was not so sure of my decision when I was still awake after a few more hours. I was very nervous and kept watching the heart rate machine all the time. It read around 60 most of the time.

Then some odd things began to happen. A man came in to visit my roommate, who was scheduled to have his surgery in the morning. He did not seem to have any visitors all the time we were together, so I was surprised when this visitor came to see him so late. As I listened in on their conversation, I found out the visitor was an insurance man from his hometown in West Virginia. I thought it was nice that he came all that way just to visit my roommate, but, as I listened more carefully, it was obvious that the man was trying to sell my roommate an insurance policy. I thought to myself, "What kind of person would be low enough to try to sell an insurance policy to a lonely man who was going to have surgery in a few hours?" The conversation got even more interesting when the visitor said, "You have to be ready in case you don't make it. If you don't have a policy, then who is going to take care of your family?" He did have a point, even though he made it rather cold-heartedly. I thought about my own situation. I certainly did not have much insurance on myself. I did not know how I would make out in my surgery. If something happened to me, what would Judy and Richie do?

As the insurance man was leaving, he stopped by my bed and asked how I was doing. I told him I would be having my bypass operation after his friend had his. He asked me if I had an insurance policy and I told him I did not. He said, "You've got to make sure you're ready to go." It sounded a little eerie as he said that, and I was in no mood to be talking about insurance at this time. I finally told him I was not interested. He accepted my answer and wished me good luck.

After he had gone, the nurse came in and put some mail on the bedside table. It was a card from my sister. I recognized the handwriting and the address on the envelope. It was a Get Well card, and she wrote some nice things on it about getting better and that she would see me the next afternoon before I went in for my bypass operation. The card was a nice gesture and I was glad that she wrote to me. But it was the little card inside that puzzled me as I read it. It was a poem talking about walking on the beach alone. It was supposed to be a card of encouragement. It sure did not sound like encouragement to me and I started to cry. Yes, I thought, I was alone all right. Why would my sister send me a card like that saying I was all alone?

After I got over the shock of what the card said, I settled down and the read the little card again. This time, I read the card all the way through, and it had a whole new meaning to me. I read the last verse in which it said that Jesus loved me and as long as I knew Him, I would never be alone. That was certainly reassuring, to know that the Lord was with me in my time of need. The poem also stated that He had already chosen me, and it was up to me to choose Him, if I so desired. The name of this little poem she enclosed was "Footprints in the Sand." It was a poem that literally SAVED my life.

FOOTPRINTS

One night a man had a dream. He dreamed he was walking along the beach with the LORD. Across the sky flashed scenes from his life. For each scene, he noticed two sets of footprints in the sand, one belonging to him, and the other to the LORD.

When the last scene of his life flashed before him, he looked back at the footprints in the sand. He noticed that many times along the path of his life there was only one set of footprints. He also noticed that it happened at the very lowest and saddest times in his life.

This really bothered him and he questioned the LORD about it. "LORD", you said that once I chose to follow you, you would walk with me all the way. But I have noticed that during the most troublesome time in my life, there is only one set of footprints. I don't understand why when I needed you most you would leave me.

The LORD replied, "My precious, precious child I love you and I would never leave you. During your times of trial and suffering, when you see only one set of footprints, it was then that I carried you."

I had known the Lord as a young boy and had accepted him as my Saviour, but I did not stay in touch with Him much. Oh, I did not rob any banks or knock anyone off. I just did not stay close to the Lord. I attended church a couple of times a year, mostly on Christmas and Easter, and even gave a few dollars in the offering. But I was beginning to think that God wanted more. Maybe He wanted a closer relationship with me.

I had thought I was alone many times in my life, but then I started thinking and mulling things over in my mind. I thought of the time my mother passed away when I was just a little lad and how my dad had kept us all together. What about the time when we moved all over the place and I was not doing well in school? Some good people came into my life and made a difference. There was the time my parents moved back to Pennsylvania, and I was on my own. The time when I lost my daughter and did not even have enough money to bury her. Why, they were even going to have to wait to bury her because the snow was so deep they could not find the plot in the cemetery. What about the time the house we wanted to rent so badly burned down, and then we found a nice little place close to work where the landlords were so good to us? The times I was able to see both my dad and mom once more before they passed away. And then the time when I pleaded with the Lord to help me get a better job so I could provide a better life for my family. When I told Him that I did not need a lot of money, and I was not afraid to work. That is when I got my good job at the Lincoln Electric Company in Euclid.

The list could go on and on of the times I prayed and the Lord intervened in my life. I certainly was not as alone as I thought I was. All those times I thought I was alone, He was right there with me. Even though I was not always there with Him, He was with me. Now I needed Him more than ever. It was about time I thanked Him from the bottom of my heart for all that He had done for me. It was time to ask Him to come into my heart again, and this time to start depending on Him.

I committed myself to the Lord again and asked Him to forgive me for all that I had done wrong. Even though I had accepted Him as my Saviour as a young boy, I considered this the time I was BORN AGAIN. I thought about the insurance man, and his words still echoed in my mind. Are you ready? Are you all set if something should happen to you? I then realized I was uncertain if I needed more life insurance as far as money was concerned, but I knew that I needed more assurance as far as God was concerned. I still think about that life insurance man and how, even though he did not sell me any insurance, he did make me think about assurance from God. Somehow, I do not think that was what he had in mind. God did sell (give) me the assurance that night that I would go to Heaven, and the only cost was that I had to ask Him to come into my heart and ask Him to forgive my sins and accept Him as my personal Saviour. All of this prepared me to go into my surgery with a peace of mind. I knew now that if things did not work out, I would be with the Lord and, in the meantime, He would be with me throughout the operation and would be with my family. Oh, what blessed assurance (insurance)!

After reading through Alice's card and poem, I noticed another envelope on the bedside table. It was a letter and, not noticing any return address on the envelope, I opened it. It looked like a somewhat short letter and was printed quite nicely. I usually do not share my personal mail with others, but I will make an exception and share this.

THE LETTER

Dear Richard,

How are you? I just had to send you a note to tell you how much I care for you and how much I LOVE you.

I saw you yesterday as you were talking with your friends. I waited all day hoping that you would want to talk with me, too. I gave you a sunset to close your day and a cool breeze to rest you—and I waited. You never came. It hurt me—but I still love you because I am your friend. I saw you sleeping last night and longed to touch your brow so I spilled moonlight upon your face. Again I waited, wanting to rush down so we could talk. I have so many gifts for you! You awoke and rushed off to work. My tears were in the rain.

If you would only listen to me! I love you! I try to tell you in blue skies and in the quiet green grass. I whisper it in the leaves on the trees and breathe it the colors of flowers, shout it to you in mountain streams and give the birds love songs to sing. I clothe you with warm sunshine and perfume the air with nature's scents. My love for you is deeper than the ocean and bigger than the biggest need in your heart!

Ask me! Talk with me! Please don't forget me. I have so much to say and share with you! I won't hassle or bother you any further. It is YOUR choice and decision. I have already chosen You and now all you have to do is choose me.

I will wait!

I love you. Your friend,
JESUS

Oh, what a letter! Between the "Footprints" poem and the "Letter" from my friend, I give credit to both of them for saving my life. I know the real credit goes to the Lord for watching over me that night and putting both the poem and the letter in my hands. I do not believe that this was just a coincidence. If I had taken the sleeping pills and the Valium, I would have fallen asleep and probably would never have read them. I probably would never even have had the chance to talk to the insurance man and the Assurance Man. Thank you, Jesus, for watching over me.

During all that transpired that night, I had kept a close watch on the monitor. It was reading in the fifties now, at about 4 or 5 in the morning. As I kept an eye on the monitor, I saw it go down into the 40's, down, down, 45, 44, 43, 42, 41, and then 40. I got scared and rang the buzzer for the nurse. When she did not come right away, I held the buzzer down without letting up on it, especially when I saw it go down even further, 39, 38—Finally, the nurse came in and asked what was wrong. I excitedly pointed to the monitor, too scared to say anything. She immediately called the doctor on duty that night in the heart ward. He came in, gave me a shot and some medicine, and then called my heart surgeon at home. He gave them some instructions over the phone, and the doctors and nurses said I would be going in for surgery at 6:00 P.M. I got on the phone to Judy and told her what was happening. She was half asleep, and I had to repeat my story several times. I told her the operating time and asked her to call my brothers and sister. My sister lived close by, but both my brothers lived out of town.

I did not know if they would come or not. Jr. lived in Andover, Ohio, and Gene lived in Linesville, Pennsylvania. There was not much they could do, but I thought they should know in case something went wrong. At least I knew that I would be on their minds anyway.

The personnel did not waste any time preparing me for surgery. I was cleaned up, had my chest shaved, given medicine to relax me, and a host of other things were done to me. Judy and Richie came in about 5:30 A.M. and sat with me while I was being prepped. The actual surgery would not take place until closer to 8:00 P.M., but I would be taken out of my room at 6:00 P.M. They wheeled me to a room just outside the operating room doors. I could never quite understand why there seemed to be so much waiting in the hospital, even before surgery. Just before I was wheeled into surgery, I looked over and saw Jr., Gene, and Alice. Of course, Judy and Richie were already there. They all gave me the thumbs up signal and, after a kiss from Judy and a hug from Richie, they wheeled me away into the operating room.

I remember talking to the anesthesiologist and his telling me to count to 100. I got to 10 and then I was out! The operation took about 5 hours. Boy, what an ordeal! I would not wish that on anybody. Obviously, it was successful, and I was so thankful that Jesus was watching over me throughout it. Next, I went to the step-down room after my surgery, and there were many other patients in there, too. I had not realized that so many people had heart operations. I was hooked up to all kinds of machines, and different tubes were dangling all over me. It was pretty scary, but at least I knew I was out of surgery. It took a while to sort things out and adjust to what was happening. All of a sudden, I seemed to be having trouble breathing and my mouth was full of spit and saliva. I motioned for one of the nurses to come over and help me, but he either did not see me or was ignoring me. I thought it was the latter. The next time he came within reaching distance, as sick as I was, I reached out and grabbed him with a death grip. There was no way this nurse was going anywhere until he helped me. I was feeling panicky because I really thought I was going to die with all that stuff in my mouth clogging my breathing. I was thinking, "I survived a heart bypass operation and now I am going to die because some nurse did not help me out and clean out my mouth." I did not let go of that nurse as he called for help and they suctioned the gunk out of my mouth. I had tubes going down my throat and nose, and that probably made the situation seem worse. I had to wait several hours before they took out the tube from my throat. It made a big difference when they did that. I could finally breathe again, but with every breath there was pain. I guess that was to be expected, considering that my chest had just been cut open from my throat to my belly button.

The doctor who operated on me was Dr. Floyd J. Lloop. He was one of the top heart surgeons in the state of Ohio and probably in the country. He is now the head of the Cleveland Clinic, I believe either the president or CEO. I know that he holds an extremely high position there. Dr. Lloop came in to check on me before I was transferred to the intensive care unit. I remember that he said, "We almost lost you." I asked him what he meant by that. He replied, "Your heart stopped for a few seconds, and I thought we would have to jumpstart you. But you came back on your own after a few seconds." That could explain why I saw this bright light and a big door barely cracked open. I thought I was dreaming, but I guess I was not. I had really seen Jesus at the door, but He would not let me in. He told me He had other plans for me and He would see me later. I did get a glimpse before the door closed, though. I guess that will be another story.

I stayed in the intensive care unit for a day or so. Judy and Richie were allowed to come in for 10 minutes at a time every 4 hours. Then I was taken to a regular room. Every day I would have to walk and exercise so I could get stronger. I finally was strong enough to go home after recuperating about 10 days in the hospital.

I went back to work about 6 weeks after my operation. I was on light duty for a month or so. The boss asked if I was ready to go back to my regular job then, but I told him I did not think I was ready yet. I was still a little anxious about trying to work that hard again. My boss said he would give me one more week and, if I was not ready then, he would have to cut my pay. I might even have to work in the cafeteria or clean the locker rooms. I would have to work for almost half of what I was earning at that time. I certainly could not afford to do that, so I went back to my old job, even though I did not feel I was ready yet. I asked the Lord to watch over me and help me get through my anxiousness. I got a little stronger every day, thanks to the Lord. As I said earlier, I had given myself to the Lord and actually went to church the first Sunday I was out of the hospital. I rely on Him more now than ever before. Thank you, Jesus.

In my prayers I have told Jesus many times how good He is and I have thanked Him hundreds of times for what He has done for me and what He means to me, especially after my heart operation. Even though there is no such thing as making deals with the Lord, I did promise Him that if He got me through my heart operation that I would thank Him for the rest of my life. The Lord has told me that He appreciates all the praises and how I feel about Him, but he has always impressed upon my heart that if think that much of Him, why don't I tell someone else about Him. I have answered back to him, "I would love to tell someone about what You have done for me, but I do not really have anyone to tell it to nor do I have anyplace to tell it." The Lord has not reminded me of my promise but has just told me that He will find people for me to tell (where two or three are gathered together) and the places to tell it. He has said that all I have to do is tell them what I think of Him. That sounded fair to me, so now the rest was up to Him.

One day in March of 1985 the pastor of the church I was attending asked me to come into his office. I could not imagine what he wanted of me. He explained that something had come up and he would not be able to preach the message on Sunday, April 14. He asked if I would be able to do the message. I asked him, "Do you mean from the pulpit on a Sunday morning service?" He replied, "Yes." That would be the Sunday after Easter, the 14th. That date was familiar to me because a year ago to the day I had my heart bypass operation. I told him I wanted to think it over for a day or so, and I would get back to him with an answer. I took it to the Lord in prayer and thought it over for a while. God reminded me that I had once said that I would tell someone how good He had been to me and what I thought about Him. I did say something like when I had my heart surgery, but I did not think that I would ever deliver that message from the pulpit to a whole congregation.

I was a little reluctant to speak that Sunday because I really did not know what I would say. And who would want to listen to what I had to say anyway? But the Lord had gotten me the audience and had found a place for me to speak, so now He told me the rest was up to me. He told me He would be right by my side, in case I faltered. I honestly did not have a choice when He put it that way. But I was still reluctant to speak and continued to make excuses. The next excuse I gave was that I only wanted to tell the story of the "Footprints" poem and the little card my sister sent me while I was in the hospital, and this would not be sufficient for a full message.

I wanted a big picture with the poem on it. My sister had one displayed in her house, and I wanted one to show to the church and present it to them. I looked around at some of the local stores and could not find one. I had made up my mind that I was not going to speak unless I found the big "Footprints" picture with the poem on it. It was then that I got a call from my niece, Anna, who is named after my real mother. "Uncle Rich!" she said rather excitedly. "I found your 'Footprints' picture." I was surprised that she found it because I had looked all over for it. That made up my mind. I now had the people to tell my story to and had a place to speak and even had my "Footprints" picture to present the church. So now I did not have any choice. After all, I did promise the Lord that each year on the anniversary of my operation that I would make a special effort to tell someone about Jesus. I told the pastor that I would deliver the message on Sunday, April 14, 1985. I have spoken to a church group every year in April since 1985. I do not just wait until April to tell people about the Lord and what He has done for me. However, that month is special to me and I treat it like another birthday because it was the month I was born again.

That Sunday I spoke at church was special to me. The church had done a little marketing for me by making some fliers and I distributed them to a few local establishments. My brothers, sister, and some of my nieces and nephews were there along with a few guests who had read the advertisements. The church's attendance was usually about 50 or so, but that Sunday we had well over 100. I presented the church with the "Footprints" picture and had a large cake made with the "Footprints" picture and its logo on it that we had with coffee after the service. To my knowledge, the "Footprints" picture is still hanging in the church near the front door.

Oh, what a blessing it was for me when, after delivering the message, I gave an altar call. This is where people come up front to pray and accept the Lord as their Saviour. I will always remember that day. Thank you, Jesus, for being there and for making my day by telling a story about You. Thank you for being there with me and guiding me with the right words to say. I am most thankful for the people who came forward.

CHAPTER 14

1987—Judy

I had regained most of my strength back, and my health was nearly back to normal by the middle of 1986. Things at home were going better, and work was rolling along pretty well, too. In December, 1986, Judy was having a lot of stomach pain. I told her she needed to make an appointment with her gynecologist. With the holidays coming on and with her doctor's schedule being so busy, she could not get in for an appointment until the first week in January of 1987. Judy kept having the severe pains all through the month of December. I suggested that she go to another doctor, but she insisted on waiting for her doctor. Her appointment finally rolled around, and she had a pap smear, some x-rays, and a sonogram. The office said they would get back to her within a few days with the results of the tests. The results were not good. There was a spot on one of her ovaries, and she was asked to come back in for more tests. A biopsy of the spot on her ovary was taken, and it resulted in more bad news. The ovary would have to be removed.

Judy had the operation at the Lake County East Hospital in Painesville, Ohio.

After I had been in the waiting room for several hours, the doctor came in and said they had removed Judy's ovary. They had gotten all the cancer, and she would be going home in a few days. Then, after a short recovery, she would be just fine. Judy was home only a month or two and started having severe stomach pains again. Another appointment and more tests showed more spots, and she had to have another operation. This time, she had a complete hysterectomy. Again, the operation was considered a success and she came home to recover again. But it was the same thing all over again—more pains, worse than ever.

This time we went to the Cleveland Clinic for another opinion in the hopes that we would get better results. After all, this was a bigger and supposedly better hospital. Her doctor at the Clinic was Dr. Webster, considered one of the best in the area for ovarian cancer. I had talked with another doctor I knew, and he had suggested Dr. Webster. When his wife had ovarian cancer a few years before, this was the doctor he took her to and who performed her operation. She was doing just great now. Since things were even more advanced now, this doctor said he would definitely recommend Dr. Webster.

After more tests were performed, Dr. Webster suggested exploratory surgery to find out what was wrong. Once Judy was opened up for the exploratory surgery, they found cancer throughout her lower stomach. The operation took a long time, 5 or 6 hours. Dr. Webster came out to the waiting room and told me the operation took a lot longer than he had anticipated and he would explain the results to me later after he got cleaned up and changed. He met with me in his office about an hour later and explained that Judy had cancer throughout her lower stomach. He felt her only chance of survival was to remove as much of the cancer as he could, so he did. That is why the operation lasted so long. He advised chemotherapy treatments for her as soon as possible.

Judy was home for only a week, and they started the chemo treatments. She would have to have a treatment every week for 20 weeks or more. Every week, I would take her in and stay with her for her treatment. In order to do this, I would have to get up at 3:00 A.M. and go to work from 4 A.M. to 8 A.M. Then I would leave work and take her to the hospital for her treatment. I never missed a treatment with her because she did not want to start it without me there holding her hand. Each chemo session would last about 3 hours. Judy would have to be sedated somewhat and would not start the chemo without my being there with her, holding her hand. When the treatment was finished, I was always still there, holding her hand. Then I would go back to work from 12:00 P.M. to 4:00 P.M., get washed up a little, go back to the hospital, and pick Judy up to take her home. The next week, it would be the same routine all over again.

There was no Family Leave Bill at that time, so I did not get any time off to be with Judy. Lincoln Electric was not too happy about the time that I did take to be with Judy, even though I worked my 8 hours every day. If the hospital bills had not been piling up and I had not needed my insurance so desperately, I would have just taken the time off to be with Judy and not thought about the consequences. But I did need my job in order to pay for the staggering hospital bills, so I continued the same crazy schedule for many weeks. The Lincoln Electric Company would have fired me for missing even a few days, let alone weeks or months. It did not matter what the problem was, there was zero tolerance for missing more than a few days of work.

Judy became sicker and sicker every day. She did have a few good days, but they were mostly bad. We did not do too much that year because she was just too sick from the chemotherapy. Before Judy became gravely sick, I asked her if she would like to have a new car so she could go places easier and not have to worry if she was very far away from home. She liked to go out to visit some of her family in Pennsylvania and she could have used a more reliable car. She also liked to bum around with her friends occasionally, going shopping and out to dinner. I was a little surprised when she said the old car was in pretty good shape and she did not see where there would be a problem in driving it for a while longer. She said, "You know what I would like to have? A family room, so I can have some of my friends over and have more room to entertain them." Judy usually did not have many people over, mostly some of the ladies from the church and some friends she had known for a number of years, but if she wanted a family room instead of a new car, then that is what she would get.

I started on the family room in April. It would be a 20'X 30' room, with part of it being a screened patio with sliding windows and doors. As Judy became more ill, I found that it had been a big mistake to try to build the room at that time. But this was what she had wanted. I did not have time to work on it, take care of her, and still go to my regular job. I tried to hire people to help me, but good help is hard to find. I practically wrote a blank check to one construction firm and told them the room had to be done in one month, regardless of how many workers they had to hire. I said if the room was not done completely in one month's time, then the company would get nothing. I handed them the contract and told them to sign if they wanted the job. They said they would get back to me in a few days. I never heard from them again.

In late October, the Cleveland Clinic called me at work and said they needed to have Judy in the hospital immediately. I went out to start my truck and, for some reason, it would not start. This was the first time the truck had ever failed to start. Even though it was an older truck, 1971, it was in perfect shape. I went back into the shop and told some of the guys my problem. I told them I was supposed to take my wife, who was getting sicker, into the Cleveland Clinic immediately. I asked if someone would take me home to get my other car or if I could borrow someone's car. The response I got astounded me. I was told, "Richard, you have worked here for over 22 years and you have gotten more than most of the people here. If you can't get to the hospital, then that's your problem." Boy, was I surprised to get an answer like that, and this response was from more than one person. What a slap in the face! The only way I was going to get home to get Judy to the hospital was to walk. I really did not mind the walk home so much (4 or 5 miles), but I was scared and in a hurry and wanted to get there as soon as possible. I would have tried to call a cab, but I was too mixed-up to do that and, besides, I only had a few dollars on me. If nobody was willing to take me home, then I doubt anyone would have lent me the money to call a cab.

I had to get home and, since I could not get any help at the shop, I headed out to Heisley Road, the main one, and stuck my thumb out at the first car that came by. I got lucky, and the guy stopped and said, "I'm only going up the road a few miles to work, but if that will help, jump in." I got settled in the car and told him my story—I only lived a few miles away but was in a hurry because my wife was supposed to go to the hospital. He worked at PolyChem, but he passed it by and continued on to Hendricks Road and turned left toward my house. He said, "I'll be a little late, but I'll get you home first." I gave him the directions, through my tears. I was taken aback by the fact that the people I had worked with for 22 years would not take me home, but a complete stranger took me out of his way straight to my door. He must have thought there was something seriously wrong with me. He pulled into the driveway and, as I got out of the car, I said, "Thanks, buddy!" and threw the few dollars that I had onto his front seat. Then I ran into the house. I never did ask that guy his name, so I have no idea who helped me that day. But I am sure Lord has it written down in the tablet where He keeps track. Thank the Lord for people like that and thank you, Jesus, for watching over me once again. Every once in a while, just when I think nobody cares, someone is there to help me. I wonder sometimes, "How does that happen????"

Once inside the house, I told Judy that the Cleveland Clinic had called me at work and she was supposed to go to the hospital A.S.A.P. They had called her, too, and she said it was not an emergency. It was just that the chemotherapy was not working and they wanted to start her on radiation right away. Judy did not want to go because she was afraid they would keep her there. There was no way she wanted to go in for an extended stay. I explained that they would do the radiation and she would be home in a day or two. I honestly thought that this was what would happen. I told her she would be home in short order. But I was wrong. Judy was in the hospital for the next 30-40 days. To this day, I still feel bad because I promised her she would be home soon and she was not. There was nothing I could do because she needed the radiation treatments. However, those radiation treatments did not help very much because Judy would not cooperate. She hated those radiation treatments!

I visited with Judy every day and still continued to go to work. My day usually went something like this: Up at 3:00 A.M., worked from 4:00 A.M. to 8:00 A.M., to the hospital for radiation treatments, back to work from 12:00 P.M. to 4:00 P.M., back to the hospital that evening. My son, Richie, was there every day with me. Boy, what a schedule! I would not wish that on anyone. It still bothers me that my boss did not cooperate with me at all. I asked him why, and he said, "A lot of the guys do not like the idea of you coming to and leaving work whenever you want, even if it is to take care of your wife." I was shocked. I could not imagine anyone getting jealous over someone taking care of his extremely ill wife. Whenever I tried talking to him and explaining the situation to him, he would say even more horrible things to me, like "Remember, your wife won't always be here, but if you want your job, you had better be." Boy, what a statement! I could not believe he had said such a thing. Later, when I said something to him about it, he said that I took it wrong and that was not exactly what he meant. I turned the statement around every which way and, to me, it said the same thing. It was a real insult It was all I could do not to take a swing at him, but I had to keep uppermost in my mind that I could not afford to lose my job. At that time, I had around $250,000.00 in hospital/doctor bills. I decided it would be better to let it go and concentrate on getting my wife better. I needed to try and get her back home. I could straighten the other stuff out later.

While Judy was in the hospital, I did not do anything on the new family room. I just did not have the time. I certainly would have liked to finish it for her, so when she came home she could enjoy it. However, Judy was not getting any better, and the hospital called me several times at night when she was not doing very well. I had told them to do this, so I would be kept up to date on her progress. One time, she was so bad that they had to bring her back after she had already slipped away. Judy did not complain much at the hospital, especially since she did not have to have the radiation treatments anymore. The one thing she did ask me was to be with her if anything happened to her. I promised that I would be there with her. That is why I gave the instructions to call me, regardless of time, if her condition worsened.

Judy did not have many visitors. The pastor of the church we attended did not even visit her, until I got upset and confronted him about this. Judy worked at the church part-time and thought so highly of this pastor. He finally did come and visit one time. He told me that he was too busy and had other things going on while Judy was so sick. Most of Judy's family did not even visit, until I finally called one of her older brothers. I told him Judy was not doing well at all and that he and the family should at least come to see her in the hospital. A few days later, her brother and a couple of her sisters came to visit. She was so happy to see them, and I was glad for her that they came. When I asked them why they had not come before, all they could respond was that they did know Judy was that sick. That was the only time they came to visit. I just do not understand things like that. It broke my heart that her family seemed so distant and uncaring.

It was now December, and Judy was in a semi-coma. I sensed that she still recognized Richie and me and knew that we were there. We continued to visit every day. On Wednesday, I left work early and went to visit Judy about 1:00 P.M. To my surprise, she was sitting up in bed and seemed to be pretty alert. She looked better than I had seen her look in the past few weeks. I sure was glad she was doing so much better. We talked and talked about all kinds of things. I let her do most of the talking, since she had not been responsive for so long. Then, all of a sudden out of the blue, she asked, "I'm not going to make it, am I?" I was so startled by what she had just asked that it took me a while to compose myself. I wondered to myself why she would say something like that when she seemed to be doing better.

The next statement she made was even more confusing to me. She said, "You know, I'm not sure I'm going to Heaven. I have some things I want to talk to you about." I was unclear about why she thought she was not ready. Judy had been saved as a young girl, and she certainly did not do anything really sinful or wrong that I knew of. She did not knock anybody off, rob any banks, do drugs, or run around. She was just a good, honest, down-to-earth kind of person. Up until 1984, she had attended church and Sunday School much more regularly than I did. Of course, I realized that just going to church was not what got someone into Heaven, but it certainly did not do any harm. She continued to talk and itemized things she had done over the years that she was sorry for. Most of the things she talked about were in the very distant past and I did not even remember half of what she was talking about. She talked about things that did not go quite right or things that she was sorry for. Most of this did not mean much to me. As far as I was concerned, there was no reason for her to say she was sorry. I had already forgotten about most of it, and it just did not matter, especially at this time. She told me she was sorry she had not always cleaned the house the way I wanted, or that she did not iron the shirt I wanted to wear that one time, or that she did not have dinner ready for me when I got home from work every time—

things that were sort of trivial as far as I was concerned. But evidently it meant a lot to her, and she needed to get it off her chest. She continued to talk, and I did not stop her. I knew she needed to get it all out.

At the time, Judy was not getting along with my sister and she told me she was sorry for the wrongs that had happened between them. She wanted to make sure I told Alice. Even though Alice and Judy had been best friends in high school and were matrons of honor at each other's wedding, somewhere along the way they had a difference of opinions. I was surprised that she brought up Alice's name, but whatever she had to say, I let her say it, regardless of how trivial it sounded to me. Today, I am so glad that I let her talk and say the things that she wanted to. We did more talking in those next few hours than we had done in many years. I am so glad that we did, and I am sure it was for a reason.

We had talked all day and most of the evening. Around 9:00 P.M. I got up to get ready to go, since visiting hours were supposed to be over at 8:00 P.M. The nurses were used to me being there late, and they never kicked me out. However, Judy said, "You're not going home already, are you? Why don't you stay a little longer?" I had already been there 7 or 8 hours, but I was ready to stay longer if she wanted me to. I thought she might be getting tired and, now that she was feeling better, she would certainly need her rest. I got a cup of coffee and sat down in a chair beside her and held her hand while we talked some more. Again, I let her do most of the talking. I could not get over how much better she seemed to be doing. Even Richie said, "Maybe mom will be coming home soon and that would be nice for Christmas." Around 11 P.M., I got up to leave since I had to be up at 3:00 A.M. for work. I told Judy that I was leaving and would be back the next day around 6:00. I gave her a kiss goodbye and, as I started to leave, she clung to my hand and said something that I will always remember, "I love you and have always loved you. I'm sorry that I didn't tell you more often and that I didn't always show you. I just had a funny way of showing my love." Her last words were: "I'll see you later." I gave her another kiss and we said our goodnights.

As Richie and I were putting our coats on at the nurses' station, we were talking about how good Judy looked and about her possibly coming home. One of the nurses heard bits and pieces of our conversation, and she made what we thought was an odd statement to us. She said, "Judy's going home, all right. It won't be long now." I could tell by the tone and inflection of her voice that she did not mean to our home in Mentor. It sounded like she did not think Judy had long to live. This puzzled me because I knew that this was the best Judy had been in a long time.

On the way home, Richie was excited and happy that his mom was doing better. He kept asking when I thought she would come home. He rattled on and on about mom being home for Christmas and how we might even put up a tree and do some shopping for her. "We'd better get the house cleaned up before mom gets home," he said. Needless to say, I had not done much cleaning while Judy was in the hospital.

Richie did not stop talking about how good mom looked and when she would be home. He sure did love his mom and missed her not being home.

We got home around midnight and I had just fallen asleep when the phone rang about 1:00 in the morning. The call was from Cleveland Clinic and I was told that Judy had fallen into another coma and was failing fast. I needed to get there as soon as possible. I woke Richie up, we got dressed, and back down to the Clinic we went. We got there about 2:00 A.M. I parked my car where the doctors parked. They had given me a special permit because I spent so much time at the hospital. I could not get through the door I usually went in, so I went around to the door that led to the kitchen. I went in through the kitchen into the hospital and was just getting on the elevator when the security guard yelled, "STOP!" I ignored him and continued onto the elevator and hit the button for Judy's floor. I did not stop for security because I knew they would ask me 20 questions and, if Judy was real bad, I might not make it there in time. I was not taking any chances. I had made a promise to her that I would be there beside her if she passed away.

Judy's room was just across from the elevator, and I was just ahead of security. I was already in her room when he got off the elevator. He came in and was going to question me, but then he saw all the doctors and nurses clustered around Judy's bed. Once he saw what was happening, he quietly left the room. The doctors and nurses had done everything to make sure Judy was comfortable, but she was so out of it that she barely knew I was there. It was so hard to believe that she had taken such a turn for the worse in such a short amount of time. When I had left only a few hours earlier, she had been doing great.

I sat with her during the rest of that night and about 6:00 A.M. her regular doctor came in and talked with me. He said Judy was failing and would not make it much longer. The staff was making her comfortable and he assured me that she was not in pain. She was on life support because, without it, she had to labor for every breath she took. It was so hard to see her this way. Always before, as I prayed for her each day, I would say: "Dear Lord, please let me spend one more day with Judy." But this day, I did not say that same prayer. I said to myself, "What am I thinking about and who am I thinking of?" I could see that I was thinking about myself in wanting to spend more time with Judy. This day my prayer was different. I asked the Lord to do what His will was. If He thought this was the day she should go home to be with Him, then I wanted His will to be done. I had always thought I was in control in some way. As long as I asked for another day, He gave it to me. It was on this day that I really turned the matter over to Him (as if He weren't already in charge). And it was then that the Lord took Judy to be with Him.

So, on December 3, 1987, at about 6:00 P.M., Judy passed away. I was there holding her hand as I had promised and as she had wanted. As sick as she had been that year, it was still hard to believe that she was gone. I called the nurses and they got a doctor to come and check her. I asked if they were going to try to bring her back, and they calmly told me, "She's gone. There's nothing more we can do." Richie was in the waiting room so I had the sad task of going to him and telling him that his mom was gone. In the meantime, the nurses fixed her up and let us in to say goodbye one more time. We stayed for a while, made what arrangements we could at the hospital, and then went home. It sure was a long ride home.

On the way home, Richie said something that took me by surprise. He said, "I know why the Lord took mom ahead of us." I responded with, "What do you mean by that?" He replied, "Mom was better prepared and ready to go to the Lord than we are. Besides, I think the Lord has other plans for us. Maybe we're not quite ready yet, or at least the Lord doesn't think so. He has other things for us to do." Then he quoted one of my favorite Bible verses, Jeremiah 29:11: "For I know the plans I have for you, sayeth the Lord. Plans for a future and a hope." I guess the Lord did have other plans for us. He certainly had other plans for Richie. I will explain some of these plans later in the book.

It was hard enough losing my wife, but the problems never seemed to stop. Let me explain. I had made arrangements with the Brunner Funeral Home to hold the calling hours there. Many people came to pay their respects, but there was one notable lack of respect shown—the pastor of the church Judy and I had been attending. He came to the funeral home, but he did not stop by to say anything to me or to view Judy. When someone asked him why he did not, his reply was, "I'm not standing in line that long to see anybody." I was really taken aback that he would say such an insensitive thing.

Judy had wanted her funeral service to be held at the Mentor Community Church of God where we had attended for quite a while. Not only that, but Judy had worked as a custodian at the church for a couple of years and was involved with some of the ladies' activities at the church and had some lady friends there. I had delivered the message at this church several times and was chairman of the board of trustees. I truly thought there would be no problem having the service here at our church instead of at the funeral home.

Was I ever shocked when I asked the pastor about having the service at the church, and he refused! I had been sensing that something was wrong before I even asked him, and his answer confirmed my suspicions. I had taken for granted that there would be no problem, but I was wrong. Again, I learned that nothing is for certain. The only One who can be counted on is the Lord. Not only did the pastor refuse to do the service but he refused to hold the service in the church. I was pretty upset and told him that it was not his decision to make. I told him it was up to the Lord first and then perhaps the trustees to decide who can use the church for a funeral. He told me to go ahead and see what the trustees had to say about it.

It was a little late by this time to make changes, especially after I had already told the funeral home that we were holding the service at the church. Plus, the arrangements were already being printed in the newspaper. I wondered what I was going to do now. I did not think too long before I decided to take it to the Lord. "Lord," I prayed, "You know what the problem is. I don't have a church to hold the service and I don't have a pastor to conduct the service for Judy. You know what my needs are. Would You please help me?"

The pastor started out by having a meeting with the trustees of the church. There were 5 trustees, two on the pastor's side for not using the church and two on my side in favor of using the church for the funeral. The pastor said, since it was a tie, he would be the tie-breaking vote. I had a copy of the bylaws of the church at hand and told him that was not what the bylaws stated. The bylaws stated that in the case of a tie the chairman of the board of trustees had the tie-breaking vote. Since I was the chairman of the trustees, I voted for using the church for the funeral. That made the final count three for using the church and two against.

The problem of using the church for the funeral was settled. Now I had to find someone to preside at the funeral service. I called several pastors in the area, but they were reluctant to do the service at a church other than their own. My sister, at that time, was attending the Painesville Assembly of God, and she asked her pastor if he could help me out. The senior pastor had previous commitments and would not be able to help, but he suggested the assistant pastor, Larry. My sister Alice talked with him and told him of the whole situation. Keep in mind that he had never met me before and, obviously, knew nothing about my wife. I gave him a call, expecting the worst. To my surprise, he listened to my plight and said he would be able to do the service for my wife.

On Monday, December 7, Pastor Larry conducted the funeral for my wife. As I went to the church the morning of the service, I remembered that I still did not have anyone to deliver the eulogy. I thought that someone should say something. I felt that I certainly had not planned things or thought things out very well, but I guess that was to be expected under the circumstances. At the church, I thought that I would give the pastor a chance to give the eulogy, but he refused to do even that. I was in a bind again and asked the Lord for help. Only a few minutes before the service started, one of Judy's friends, a black lady named Patsy Patterson, came in. I immediately thought I would ask her to say something about Judy. If she did not want to, I decided that I would just say something myself. When I asked her, Patsy immediately said she would be honored. to say something about Judy. Boy, that was great! My prayers were answered. I noticed that the first thing Patsy did was bow her head and ask the Lord for guidance in knowing what to say that would not only compliment Judy but also touch someone's heart attending the service. She did an excellent job in accomplishing both goals. The Lord sure did answer a lot of prayers that day. Thank you, Jesus, for answered prayers and thank you, Patsy, for your eulogy of Judy.

The idea of the pastor not helping me was hard to understand, and it really bothered me later. Since then, I have learned of some of the problems concerning him. He was not only the pastor of our church, but he was also a marriage counselor for Judge Ross D'Avelone's domestic relations court. At that time, he was very involved with one of the clients he was counseling and had no time to do any part of the service for Judy. He also was in the process of relocating to another church and, when that fell through, he was then let go as pastor of the Mentor Community Church of God. It is possible that he let his counseling job get in the way of his pastoring. I do not believe he is pastoring any church at the present time. One thing I learned from this experience is that I needed to let go and move on, no matter how hard it was for me to understand why this pastor treated me so poorly at the most difficult time in my life.

I have had such a hard time grieving and getting over the loss of my wife. We had been so young when we got married and, because of our extreme youth, many thought the marriage was doomed from the start. Especially after the loss of our baby daughter. Statistics show that about 75% of all teenage marriages end in divorce, and 75% of all couples who lose a child will also divorce within 5 years. Statistics also show that 75% of all couples with a special needs child will divorce within 5 years. Here Judy and I were, with two children and losing one, and I was only 21 years old and Judy was only 19. With the help of the Lord and with lots of prayers, we were married for 27 years. As I said before, I married Judy when she was only 17 years old. She graduated from high school one week and we were married the next. Judy was sick for about a year and in the hospital for 79 days. She had 4 or 5 operations and passed away at

44 years of age with ovarian cancer. I cannot help but think that since we had been married so young and with a little longevity, we could have been married 50 years quite easily. But that was not meant to be. As the old saying goes, "You don't miss what you have until it is gone!" So true. I certainly did take a lot of things for granted and, you better believe, I would do a lot of things differently today.

Thank you, Jesus, for saving Judy. She is now reunited with our baby girl Debbie in Heaven.

CHAPTER 15

After Judy

It was now 1988 and I had gone back to work. Soon after returning to work, my boss at the Mentor plant gave me my evaluation and grading for the previous year. I had already gotten my bonus check, which had been mailed to me, and I had noticed that the amount was far short of what I had expected. But I waited until I got back to work to see how my evaluation went before I would question the amount. After I received the results of my evaluation, I understood why my check seemed so small. I had been cut in the grading system by over 25%! When I asked my boss why I had been cut so much, his reply stunned me: "That's because your wife died. You shouldn't have defied the system and just come and gone as you pleased. You let down a lot of your co-workers, and they complained about your making your own hours and doing as you pleased without telling them more about your circumstances." I was at a loss for words and could not understand why people whom I had worked with for so many years would complain because I was trying to take care of my dying wife. I am sure no one would want to change places with me, and I wondered what any of them would do under similar circumstances. It hurt me that people would say these things about me, but there was no use wondering about why they felt that way because there was nothing I could do about it. I did talk with upper management about this situation, but they backed up what the foreman had said. That was standard policy and there was no way I was going to buck the system without losing my job. The attitude of the company was that "the door swings both ways." In other words, if I did not like it, I could move on out the door.

It did bother me that my boss claimed to be a Christian and had said those things to me. I knew that it was not for me to judge and decide whether he was a Christian or not. I will leave that up to Someone who is a better Judge than I and who will certainly make it fair for all concerned. I did know one thing, though, and that is that I would never work for that boss again. I told him exactly that. I also told him I was going back to the Euclid plant to work. He told me I could not choose where I worked and that I was not going anywhere.

A few days later, I went back to the Euclid plant to work. I reported to my old boss, Donald Elfin, and asked him where he wanted me to work and what he wanted me to do. He assigned me another job, with no questions asked. I am pretty sure that he knew I had not been treated right during my wife's illness and was willing to let things go on as they were in the hopes that I would not say anything more and make a scene. A few years later, the Family Leave Bill passed and this forever changed the way companies treated their employees when there was a catastrophic illness in the family. I am sure that many people across this nation of ours had been treated as poorly as I was, or even worse, by their employers. The needs of people are now understood better, and employees will no longer tolerate the insensitivity by employers, especially the companies which have unions. The Lincoln Electric Company still does not have a union, so they do pretty much what they want.

Things had smoothed out a work quite a bit, but I was still having great difficulty in getting over my wife's death. I did not have anyone to talk to except my son Richie, and I had to keep reminding myself that he had lost his mom and was grieving just like me. A few people at work would listen a little, but no one really wanted to hear about it. I honestly think that most people just do not know what to say to a grieving person and are either afraid of hurting feelings or of saying the wrong things.

Even my family did not know what to say or how to help me deal with Judy's death, so they just did not come around too much or say anything. All I wanted was someone to acknowledge my loss and at least be there to listen when I needed to talk. Just to receive a touch or to feel that someone cared would have meant the world to me. I suppose it was hard to understand what I was going through if someone had not already been there. All I wanted was for someone to be there for me. Anyone who has lost someone could understand that. A phone call would have been nice, or maybe even a card in the mail. An invite for dinner would have been a treat, especially since I was not a very good cook and got tired of eating out and/or eating at fast food restaurants. My experience has been that nothing needs to be said, but just being there with people who are grieving and listening to them helps more than anything.

Around this time, shortly after my wife's death, I saw an ad in the newspaper for a grief class sponsored by a local church. I did not think too much about the class until the following day when I received two cards in the mail regarding this same class. Even though people may have felt too uncomfortable to talk with me about my grief, they at least recognized my need for help in this area. So I took this as a sign that the Lord wanted me to attend the grief recovery class advertised. It was for widows and widowers and was offered by the Willoughby Hills Friends Evangelical Church in Willoughby Hills, Ohio. The class had a name: A New Beginning. I certainly needed something new, since things were not going very well for me.

The first evening I attended the class I noticed some odd coincidences. I was the first one there, except for a couple of ladies named Debbie and Janet, who were the co-facilitators. Both of them had lost their husbands a year or two before, and this was the second class they had held. The next person who came in was a man named Ray. Just as soon as we saw each other and introduced ourselves, we knew that we had met somewhere before, but it took a little time figuring out where. We talked for a while, as other people came in, and then the class started. When the lady got up and introduced herself as Debbie (my daughter's name) and told us that her husband had passed away December 3, 1986 (December 3 was the same day my wife passed away), I knew that this was the place for me to be. Already there were connecting circumstances to events in my own life.

The class proved to be just what I needed and was a big help to me. It gave me the chance to talk with others who had lost their spouses, too. I made friends with some people in that first class whom I am still in contact with today. We met every other week for almost a year. We talked on a variety of subjects relating to grief. After attending this class and seeing how it helped me and others going through the same kind of grief, I was convinced that there was no shortcut around this thing called grief. The only way to do it was to go right straight through it, facing it head-on. That was exactly what I did. I will be the first to say that I would not be in the position I am today without having gone through this class first and without having been a Christian and relying on the Lord for strength, understanding, and guidance.

After that first year of the class, we had a potluck dinner the last evening we met. All throughout 1988 I had met and talked to many people within the confines of this wonderful class. It was going to be hard to let these people go, now that the class was over. Everyone had become like family to me. Especially the guy named Ray.

Let me explain about Ray. After the class was over that first night, I stayed after for a while and talked to Ray. I found out that we both lived in Mentor, and he had lost his wife to cancer about the same time my wife had passed away. He was having trouble grieving over the loss of his wife, and he thought that the grief class might help him. He did not belong to the Willoughby Hills church where the class was held, but he had heard about the class through others, just as I had. As we were talking, we both finally remembered why we looked so familiar to each other. The year before we had lost our wives, we had attended a Bill Glass evangelistic crusade at one of the school stadiums in Willoughby. Ray and his wife had sat right in front of Judy and me. We had not said too much to each other, except for a casual hello. The crusade had lasted for about a week, and Judy and I attended three times. Each time we were there, Ray and his wife were there, too, and they always seemed to sit close to us. We did not speak but we always exchanged waves, and that was it. The next time I saw him was in the grief class. Neither of us had known that the other's wife was sick. It was so strange that each of our wives was sick at the same time, but we never said anything about it to each other during their illnesses.

Ray and I became very good friends and visited at each other's homes for prayer and to support each other. After about a year or so, we decided to go to a singles' dance that was held in the area. Ray was Polish and loved to dance. I did, too, but I was a little reluctant to go because it had only been a year and a half since my wife had passed away. He talked me into it by saying that it would be good for us to get out and do something for a change. So we ended up going to that dance and then to many other dances throughout the year. Ray met a lady named Charlotte at one of the dances. She had lost her husband about the same time we had lost our wives. Ray and Charlotte dated for a year or so, and I could see that they were an "item," as they spent more and more time together. I was pretty much on my own again.

A year or so later, Ray called and told me they were going to get married. I congratulated him and he surprised me by asking if I would be his best man. I had been an usher before at a few weddings, but I had never been best man for anyone. I thought it was great that Ray and Charlotte were getting married. They had a beautiful church wedding and a nice reception. They both sold their homes and built a new one together in Parma. They have been married for 10 years now and are doing great. They do lots of traveling and they still go dancing. Both are retired now and they have plenty of time to do some of the things they have always wanted to do. I visit them once in a while and we exchange Christmas cards. We met in some unusual circumstances and we still remain good friends.

The following year, after attending the grief class, I wanted to give something back to people who had lost a loved one like I had, and I volunteered to help at the grief class. I started out by reciting a poem that I had put together and then I became a facilitator in the different classes being held. Instead of just having a class for widows and widowers, there were now classes for anyone who had lost a loved one.

I usually facilitate the class for those who have lost a spouse, and I am now one of the featured speakers. I usually speak on the subject: Where is God in all this grief? I have worked with this class for about 12 years now. I have been blessed many times over by simply trying to help others who are grieving.

I have made so many friends in the process. Some of my "students" have remained my good friends and I have even attended some of their weddings. Such a blessing and an honor to have been invited to these happy events.

On the home front, Richie had decided it was time to go out on his own. He said, "Dad, it looks like you are doing okay now, and I think it is time for me to move on." He was 27 years old, and I agreed with him that it was time to let him go. He had wanted to leave before but, when Judy got sick, he stayed to help. He really was a big help during Judy's illness and in the years following. If nothing else, he would always listen to me, and he never complained, even though he missed his mother very much. He could have stayed with me as long as he wanted but, as I thought about it, I was not always going to be there for him. He needed to be on his own and learn about life in the real world. I wanted him to be able to self-sufficient and manage for himself. It seemed to me like he knew his way around and knew how to do things better than I did. I wanted to make sure that if something were to happen to me that he would be able to take care of himself.

In 1991, I decided to do something that I had wanted to do since I was a young boy. I was determined to run a marathon, 26 long miles. I had trained three times before but, because of different circumstances in my life, I was not able to compete. The first time was in 1983-84 when I had my heart surgery and then in 1987-88 when Judy became ill and passed away. In 1990, I had trained really hard and was all set to run the marathon when I found out I had a hernia. I still wanted to run, but the doctor advised me against it, saying that if the hernia ruptured while I was running I could possibly die. I followed my doctor's advice and did not run that year.

I had the hernia operation later that year, and then started training for the Cleveland Revco Marathon for 1991. The first thing I had to do was lose weight. Since Judy had passed away, I had gained weight from eating out too much and not watching what I was eating. I started to watch my diet carefully and managed to lose 40 pounds. I was ready to train rigorously by the spring of 1991. I ran every day and followed a training program I had seen in a runner's magazine.

Before I knew it, Sunday, May 19, arrived, and it was time to run the marathon. By that time, I had lost another 20 pounds and was in the best shape of my life, at least since high school. It was a beautiful morning to run. I had a great time talking to people as I ran. Keep in mind that I was not trying to set any records. I just wanted to finish the race, so I did a lot of talking as I ran along. It helped me pace myself. Even though 26 miles was a long way, I knew that my time for finishing the race was not as important as just plain old finishing. I could care less about my time, I just wanted to have fun doing it.

There were several top-notch athletes from around the world who ran in this marathon. Only two or three runners from the United States finished in the top ten, and it was quite a ways down the list before someone from Ohio finished. I did not have any trouble until I got to about the 22 or 23-mile marker coming across the Detroit Superior bridge. The wind was blowing so hard that I was almost at a walk. It was then that I asked the Lord to help me across that bridge and to finish the race running. As in everything else in my life, I had to finish the race that I started. The last couple of miles were the hardest. I was not so tired, but I started having pain in my right hip. I knew that if I could just get across this bridge, I could make it. I had come too far not to finish. My prayers were answered as I finally had the finish line in sight. I was so close now that I would crawl across the line if I had to.

I finished the race in a little over 4 hours, a pretty respectable time. I finished in about the middle of all the runners in my age group. Thousands of people ran in this race, and there were hundreds in my age group. As I crossed the finish line, my sister Alice and brother-in-law Lloyd and some friends were waiting there for me. It was such a happy day in my life. I even held a picnic-party in the park after the race was over to share my happiness in completing the marathon with some of my relatives and friends. Thank the Lord for healing my heart and helping me through my grief and finishing the race.

CHAPTER 16

My Brother, Jr.

It was in the fall of 1992 when I got a call at home saying that my brother, Jr., was in the hospital. I was given no explanation, except that Jr. was not feeling well and was tired all the time. I could understand why Jr. might be so tired as he worked many long hours, sometimes 16 hours a day for several days in a row. I thought he probably needed a good rest and, if he were at home, he would not get it because he always had to be doing something. Maybe a thorough checkup and a short stay in the hospital would give him the rest he so badly needed. I did not think there was anything seriously wrong with him. After all, he was only 55 years old and had never been sick that I knew of.

I decided I would go to the hospital and see for myself exactly what was wrong with Jr. I went to the hospital and, to my surprise, I had a little trouble getting in to see him because I was told that visiting was for the immediate family only. I thought I was immediate family, but evidently not, because I was not allowed in to see him. I was getting a little panicky because I figured something must be terribly wrong. I just happened to run into Mary Jayne, Jr.'s wife, in the halls of the hospital and she was very surprised to see me. Someone else had told me that Jr. was in the hospital, and she must have wondered how I knew he was there. I convinced Mary into letting me go to Jr.'s room and see him for myself. Even though he was in a regular room, I was still thinking the worst because of my not being able to see him and visit with him.

When I finally walked into his room, Jr. was sitting up in bed. I reached over and shook his hand and asked him how he was doing. He said he was fine and they just wanted to run some tests. He said he had been getting very tired and seemed to be rundown. He said, "I'm glad Mary got hold of you to let you know I was in the hospital." I did not tell him that Mary was not the one who had called me. He seemed to be doing okay, and I stayed and visited with him for a while. As I got ready to leave, Mary walked out with me. She told me that Jr. had some form of leukemia or cancer where his white or red corpuscle count was low. (It was eventually diagnosed as bone cancer.) The only form of treatment was to give him a blood transfusion.

Jr. had the blood transfusion and was in the hospital for a week or so before he was sent home. He was anxious to get back to work since he was feeling much better, but the doctors told him he could not. He needed to rest for a few weeks and then his blood count would be rechecked. A few weeks later, he seemed rundown and tired again, so he had to go back to the hospital. It was the same story again—his red or white corpuscle count was off—and he had to have transfusions again. After the transfusions, he would always feel better for a couple of weeks, and then he would start getting tired and rundown again, even though he was resting constantly.

Jr. just wanted to feel good enough to go back to work. He loved his job and was a full-blown workaholic. One of the times he was in the hospital for one of his transfusions, he asked the doctor when he would be able to go back to work. The doctor answered him without hesitation, "You have worked your last day. You will not be able to return to work." Even though Jr. was sick, I was surprised that the doctor answered him like that. He seemed to be better every time he had a blood transfusion and, once he got his red and white blood count straightened out, I really thought he would be okay and be able to go back to work. The doctor knew all along that Jr. would not go back to work. The time between blood transfusions became closer and closer. In February, he had a mild stroke, on top of the leukemia. He had trouble thinking clearly and communicating. He was doing so much worse, and it was then that I knew this was really serious.

I thought Jr. would have a better chance of recovery if he only had better care and some other opinions. It certainly would not make anything worse, so I talked to Mary about this and convinced her to take him to the Cleveland Clinic. He got a little better for a while, but then he contracted some kind of parasites and it went to his brain. His memory kept getting worse and his thinking and speech were deteriorating rapidly as time went on. I visited him several times in the hospitals and, eventually, they told him there was nothing else they could do for him. By this time, all Jr. wanted to do was to go home, so Mary had him put in the nursing care center in Andover, Ohio.

The nursing home was located just a few miles away from where they lived. I visited him there, too, and we would sit and talk. I would push him around the home in his wheelchair. During my visits, he would always say that he wanted to go home. His speech was not too clear and it was hard to understand him. Evidently, I was not thinking too well myself because it took me a while to realize that, when he said he wanted to go home, he meant he wanted to go home to his own house. He had been saying it plainly enough, but I had misinterpreted what he meant. He finally was able to come home to his own house and seemed to be doing better. I stopped and visited him at home and, one time, we even played some checkers. For one particular game, I set up my checkers so that he jumped 5 or 6 at one time and, of course, he won that game. He was so excited and yelled out, "I beat you!" He then realized that I had let him jump my men on purpose and he got very upset, saying, "You don't have to let me win. I can win on my own." That was how Jr. was. He did not want anyone to give in any at all. He was a fierce competitor and ordinarily could have beaten me most of the time. I had not meant to make him mad. I just wanted him to win, just like old times.

That summer our nephew, Bill, got married, and Jr. was able to attend. By this time he was pretty much bedridden. One thing I always respected and appreciated was that, when I visited Jr., Mary Jayne would let me go into the bedroom and sit, talk, and visit with Jr. without being interrupted. Even though I could not always understand him clearly, I do not think he understood me too well either. It was on the Sunday before he passed away that he seemed more alert. We talked quite a while and he seemed to understand and follow what I was saying. We talked about some pretty important things that day.

We were talking about heaven, and Jr. asked me about my death experience while I was having heart surgery. He asked, "Did you see any Model A Fords in heaven?" I did not quite know how to answer this. Jr. loved old antique cars, especially Model A Fords, and owned quite a few of them. He did not have any of them restored, but I suspect he had always planned to restore them after he retired. I did not want to take too long in answering him, because it might seem like I was giving a dishonest answer.

The near-death experience he was talking about was the time I got a glimpse of heaven in 1984 during my heart operation. We had talked about this experience before, but we had never talked about whether there were any Model A Fords there. However, this time he seemed pretty serious, and I had to give him a quick answer. "Sure, there are," I told him. "How else would God want us to get around except in a Model A Ford?" I was thinking to myself, "Now why did I give him a silly answer like that?" He could see that I was a little put off by the answer I had given him. He said, with a smile on his face: "I know there aren't any old cars in heaven. I was just testing you to see what kind of answer you would give me." That was certainly a relief to me because I did not want to tell him and out-and-out lie about what was in heaven according to what I had seen that day.

He went on to say: "That won't make any difference anyway, because there will be so many other things to do. We'll let the old cars stay here to give you something to look at and enjoy. I'll have plenty of things to do and a lot of catching up to do with mom and dad. I'll have things to say to Judy and even get a chance to see baby Debbie. I'll be the first one to see our baby sister who died at birth. I have lots of questions for Jesus, too, so I'll keep busy. I won't have time to fool around with old cars." I thought for a while longer and came to the conclusion that I had no idea if there were any old cars in heaven. Just because I had not seen any in my experience did not meant there were none. I guess I will not really know until I get there.

We continued to talk about many other things. He was a little apologetic, somewhat like Judy had been talking to me right before she passed away. It had been such a long time that I had carried on a lengthy conversation with him, I just let him say what he wanted to. He was sorry for not having come to see me run the marathon and to the little party afterward. He said he was too busy at the time and had lots of other things to do. He mentioned the time he had come to the Cleveland Clinic but did not stay to see Judy or me. At that time, Judy was being operated on, and they had called me to be with her as soon as they were done. I did not have or take time to speak with Jr. at that time. I went right to the room in case something went wrong during the operation. Rather than wait to see what was happening, Jr. decided to go home since he had a lot to do.

Jr. also talked about not visiting me after Judy passed away. He worked 16 hours a day much of the time and could not make time to come up to see me. All of these things seemed irrelevant to me now, but it meant a lot to him to talk about these things that day. When I finally got up to go, he stuck out his hand to shake mine. Although he was right-handed, his right hand was so sore to touch that he offered me his left hand. He still had quite a grip and squeezed my hand rather hard (all three of us boys always had a good, firm handshake) to say goodbye. He then ruffled my hair and said, "Take care of yourself. I love you, and I'll see you later." That would be the last thing he ever said to me. I told him, "I love you, too. Thanks for all you have done for me. I'll see you later."

Although we had always loved each other as brothers, Jr. and I had never told one another or spoken it before. Our family was not one to say the word "love" very often. I had always assumed that we all loved each other and did not have to say it, especially us boys. Whoever heard brothers say they loved each other? It was a shame that Jr. and I waited over 50 years to say we loved each other. How sad it was that we could not say those three little words to each other before. I learned my lesson, though. Today, I tell my family that I love them whenever I can.

Although I did not want to admit it, I knew that Jr. would not be with us on earth very much longer. I have thanked Mary personally before for letting me spend time with Jr., especially that day, and I would like to thank her again. That time together meant the world to me.

On Wednesday, November 24, Mary called me at work and told me that Jr. had passed away that morning. The next day was Thanksgiving Day. In spite of Jr.'s passing away on the day before Thanksgiving, I could not help but say thanks to the Lord for having a brother like Jr. He meant so much to my brother, sister, and me. He will be surely missed by his wife, children, and all our family. Jr. was not only respected by all of our family but by the hundreds of friends and people with whom he had come into contact.

I was honored when Mary Jayne and his children asked if I would deliver the eulogy at his funeral. Here are some of the things I said about my brother, Jr., that day: Even as a young boy, Dorrance (Jr.) was a no-nonsense kid, probably because he had to grow up a little sooner than most. When my mother passed away so young, Jr. took over and took care of the rest of us kid while my dad was working. My dad had put him in charge, quite a responsibility for a 9-year-old. Gene was seven, I was five, and Alice was three. Jr. had a way of telling us what to do and keeping us together without being bossy. At age nine, he was already a leader. We never talked about this too much as we were growing up, but we knew in the back of our minds what he had done for us. Even though my dad never mentioned it either, he knew that he had a special son. While we were growing up, Jr. never gave our dad or mom any problems like Gene, Alice, and me. Everyone he came into contact with respected him. We would never have been able to stay together if it had not been for his part in taking care of us.

He was a good husband, father, grandfather, brother, and son. He was such a good worker, almost to the extreme. He was a leader in the community, involved with his church, and manager in Little League baseball with his sons. Most of us knew of his love for old cars, especially Model A Fords. He took pride in his home and was always mowing the yard and keeping it up. He was an avid gardener, and his roots of being raised on a farm and by a farmer never really left him.

Those were some of the general things I shared about him that day. Then I shared what he meant to me personally. He always set a good example for me and always encouraged me to do well. He told me to do the best that I could and then to try a little harder. He encouraged me in school, not only in my studies but in sports, too. He was an honor student himself in high school and he expected me to do better than he did, all the while setting a shining example for me. After I graduated from high school, he continued to encourage me.

It seemed that my oldest brother was always paving the way for me when it came to jobs. My first job was at Shellito potato farms where Jr. had worked for a number of years. I then followed him to his place of employment and got my first real job at Andover Industries in Andover, Ohio. He worked there about five years and then got a job at General Motors in Warren, Ohio. That had always been his dream to work at General Motors since he was an avid Chevy man. Except for his Model A Fords, he always drove a Chevy. He started there on the ground floor, one of the first hundred people hired.

When Jr. got that good job at Chevy, it just continued to encourage me to get something better, too. I did not follow him this time, though, but I went to Cleveland, Ohio, and got a job at the Lincoln Electric Company in 1965. That did not stop me from getting together with Jr. as often as I could over the next 28 years. We were both busy working long hours and raising our families. Even though he did not come up my way to visit often, I always managed to visit him. Today, I am so thankful that I took the time out of my life's schedule to spend with him.

Jr. was never one to lie or exaggerate stories, so it meant a lot to me when he kept encouraging me and told others that I did better in school and was able to play sports better than he could. He would always brag on me to other people and tell them what a good job I had and lived in an expensive home in Mentor. He would go on and on, bragging about me. But let me set the record straight. I could never come close to doing what my brother did in his life. He had a better job, was a better worker, had a nicer home, was more intelligent, and was much stronger than me. I could go on and on about Jr.'s successes and attributes.

When my daughter passed away in 1964 and I had to move on the spot, Jr. offered his home to my family and me until we could find a place to live. At that time, I did not even have enough money to buy flowers for my daughter's funeral. Guess who took care of that for me? My brother, Jr., did. I paid him back a year or two later, but never once did he ask for the money. He knew that when I got back on my feet, he would get the money back. He surely did help me get through that terrible time in my life. He always helped, especially when times were tough. I surely do miss him and always remember and be thankful for all he did for me. I could write a book about Jr., but this will have to do for now. Thank you, Jesus, for giving me such a brother, friend, and mentor. I love you, Jr.

CHAPTER 17

My Brother, Gene

During the time that Jr. was sick, my other brother, Gene, was diagnosed with prostate cancer. That was in 1993. To have both brothers sick at the same time was hard to understand. Gene had gone to the hospital for tests and they thought they would remove his prostate. When they opened him up for the operation, the doctors found that the cancer was too rampant, so they closed him back up and decided to use medicine to fight the cancer. He had plenty of chemotherapy and radiation treatments, which seemed to put the cancer into remission.

At his 55th birthday party in October, Gene said to me, "Are you going deer hunting with me this year, or are you going to give me some excuse again and not go?" I told him I would go hunting with him for sure this year, no excuses. He did not quite believe me and said, "You've been telling me that for years and years, and you have not gone with me once." I repeated that I would go hunting with him. I knew in my heart that it would be different that year and that I would go with him. Now that he was sick, I would have to keep my promise to go. Gene was so excited about going deer hunting and, whenever we saw each other, that was all he would talk about. He even called me several times, just to make sure that I had not changed my mind.

Jr. passed away the week before deer season started but, with mixed emotions, I kept my promise and went deer hunting with Gene for the first time. I knew that Jr. would have wanted us to go hunting. I could visualize him looking down on us as we were hunting, almost like we were all together again. It would have been nice for all three of us to have hunted together, but, since that was not to be, I could and would go hunting with Gene. Gene sure did like to hunt his deer.

I went out to Gene's the night before the first day of deer hunting season. Gene was so happy and could hardly believe that I was really going hunting with him. He let me use the gun he had shot his first deer with and, to be honest with you, all of his children got their first deer with the same gun. Even some of his grandchildren had used the same gun to go hunting and get their first deer. That gun had a lot of history.

When Gene had said I was going hunting with him, I took him literally and thought he meant that I would be by his side or at least close to him while we were hunting. I sure had that wrong. After walking into the woods for a mile or so, he pointed out a spot for me to stand and said he was going farther into the woods and would see me later. Gosh, I did not have any idea where I was and I do not think I could have found my way out by myself if I had tried. Gene had gone farther into the woods and I was completely alone. I do not mean to sound like a sissy, but it was dark and I had no idea where I was. I did see some other hunters go by me with their flashlights on, and I waved my light so they would know where I was.

Once it got light out, it was not so bad, but I still did not know where Gene was. I was pretty naïve when I thought he would stick with me and stay close but, as I soon found out, that "just isn't how you go deer hunting." I did see some does go by, but I was in buck country and could not shoot a doe. I had heard lots of shooting all around me, but I did not see any buck deer.

Later on that morning, I heard a couple of shots that were pretty close. I heard Gene yell, "Over here, Rich! I think you got one!" I thought to myself, "What does he mean 'I think you got one'? I haven't even taken a shot yet." I left my station and headed toward his voice. Sure enough, there he was with not one, but two, buck deer. "How did you get two bucks?" I asked. He said, "Oh, I shot this other one by mistake. Do you want to tag it?" I thought for a moment and said, "No, I want to get one on my own and by myself." I figured it was only the first day of deer season and, since I would be off all week, maybe I would see one later. I helped Gene field dress his deer and then we had to drag it through the creek and up over the bank. I had my camera with me and took a couple of pictures. One turned out to be a really nice picture and is one of my favorite pictures of my brother, Gene. By the way, some other guy came through and Gene convinced him that the other deer was his.

I did not see any more deer that day and, now that Gene had his limit, he would not be out in the woods so much, at least not at 6:00 in the morning. My niece and nephew, Sandy and John Tracy, have a small farm around Meadville, Pennsylvania, so I decided to go there to hunt on their property. I thought I would be able to hunt better there because on their farm I could shoot a buck or a doe. The rules for hunting were not as rigid there. I really did not care what I got, just so I got something. I saw lots of does that day, but I could not get a good shot at any. How had Gene shot two bucks at one time? I had not even seen a buck yet. Maybe I did not have enough patience.

The next day, Wednesday, I went to the same spot where I had seen the deer the morning before. Sure enough, they came out at about the same time, and I was ready this time. There were five does in one herd and I had to decide which one to shoot. My brother had always told me to look them over and shoot the biggest one. By that time, they had all seen me and they were moving out. I did not have much time to pick out a big one. I just shot the first one I could get into the sight of my gun. BAM! I let go with a shot and, to my surprise, the deer fell over. Now I was a little nervous and did not quite know what to do. I did not think I would be this nervous and that there would be such a rush. I saw my nephew, John, over in another stand and waved him over. He helped me field dress the deer, and then we went to get his Chevy Blazer and we drove right up through the field. We threw the deer into the back of the Blazer and headed down to the house. That was a lot easier than with Gene's deer. We had to drag his deer over a mile through the woods and out to the road where his truck was parked.

After hanging the deer up, I could not wait to get into the house and call to tell Gene my deer story. There really was not much to the story, but I acted like most hunters do and embellished it a little. It must have taken me an hour to tell him all about getting the deer. I even got the deer with the same gun that he got his first one with. I only wish he could have been there with me when I shot my first deer. He had not been feeling too well because the treatments he was getting for his cancer were making him very tired. But less than a half hour after I had talked to him on the phone, here came Gene into the driveway to see the deer I had got. He was just as happy as I was. He almost acted like he was there with me when I shot it. That was a day I will never forget. I was now hooked on deer hunting and would hunt with (or around) my brother for the next seven years, getting a deer every year.

During the first six years of being sick, Gene's cancer was in remission and he went hunting every year. I still had not actually gone hunting with him, but we hunted in the same vicinity several times. In 1998, he got a nice 8-point buck and had it mounted. It was one of the nicest bucks he had ever gotten in his lengthy hunting career. I still had not gotten a big buck yet. All mine were what they call "button bucks", ones with wee little antlers.

In 1999, Gene's cancer returned full force, and he was pretty sick most of the year. He was still looking forward to hunting that winter, but he was not getting around too well as hunting season approached. So that fall his sons and daughter, along with some of Gene's deer hunting buddies, built him a special deer stand. I called it "the deer stand made out of love." It was a big stand with lots of room and mostly closed in. It had a roof on it, a couple of chairs and even a heater in it. It was almost like being in the house. (Ha, ha) They had hung all kinds of deer pictures in it, and that made it real homey for Gene. His loved ones had also built a staircase up to the stand, about 20 feet in the air. That made it a little easier for Gene to get up in the stand.

The day before hunting season started that year, I went to John and Sandy's to stay and scope things out. Actually, it was the first time I had seen Gene's new stand. Boy, was it nice! Even better than I had thought it would be. Gene had told me about the stand during one of our phone calls. I used to call to see how he was doing, but all he would talk about was going hunting with me.

Well, the morning of deer season had finally come. Everyone was up at 5:00 A.M., even though the actual time to start hunting was 7:00 A.M. We all had breakfast and coffee and talked about the big buck we were going to get. Shortly after six, we started dressing into our hunting gear. Gene's stand was only about a half mile from the house through the woods, but he was dressed and ready to go. He had a four-wheeler there to ride, because he was unable to walk to the stand. The others had cut a nice path to the stand, even though it was through the woods.

Everyone was ready. Gene had the four-wheeler running and was waiting as I walked from the driveway, headed toward my stand. He said to me, "Where are you going? Aren't you hunting with me?"

He had said the same thing the previous seven years, but I had never really hunted with him—I mean side-by-side in the same stand. I was still somewhat puzzled as he said, "Hop on. I'm ready to go." I got on the back of the four-wheeler and away we went. He had little trouble driving and took his time. He knew right where he was going. It only took us a few minutes to get to the newly built stand, and he was able to drive right to the stairs leading up to the stand.

As we got ready to climb the stairs, he handed me his gun and said, "You had better carry this. I will need both hands to hold onto the railing." I waited for him to go up the steps but could see that he was having a little trouble. So I put the guns down on the four-wheeler and helped him up the stairs. I could not believe that, as sick as he was, Gene still wanted to hunt. I was getting a little emotional and was starting to cry. I could not help it. Gene turned partly around and said, "What's wrong with you? Stop the crying and get me up the stairs." I got him up the stairs and settled into one of the chairs there. Through all the commotion of helping him up the stairs and getting him settled in, he kept telling me to be quiet or I would scare all the deer away. I went back down the stairs and got the guns.

By the time I got back up the steps, I had composed myself and got settled in the other chair. It was still dark but, as light was approaching, Gene gave me advice from his store of hunting expertise and told me where and how to look and watch for the deer. He seemed to know intuitively where the deer would be coming from. He had shot three or four deer from the previous stand before they took the old one down and built the new one, so he knew what he was talking about.

Usually Gene was quiet as a mouse when hunting, but this time he was very talkative. He did not talk loudly, but he definitely wanted to talk. We still looked out for deer, but that did not keep us from talking. It reminded me of the conversation I had with Jr. when he just kept talking about all sorts of things. Gene surprised me when he asked, "Do you think there are any deer in heaven and I'll be able to hunt?" Boy, that was a hard one to answer, just as Jr.'s Model A Ford question was. I decided to be a little more honest this time. I remembered the song we sang a lot at church about how "the deer panteth for the water." I was not quite sure what that song meant, but I told him, "The deer are there to watch and just to look at. It will be so peaceful that you will just want to enjoy them. You'll be able to pet them and play with them, like pets." Just like Jr., he said, "Boy, that would be great! I won't be hunting anymore. I was just kidding you, but I sure would like to see deer in heaven." Today, I can just envision Jr. driving Gene around in his Model A Ford, looking for deer.

Gene had not been saved too long, as my sister had led him to the Lord only a few months earlier, but he was eager to talk about the Lord and things that had bothered him throughout his life. Again, I did not stop him and let him talk about anything he wanted. It made me a little nervous, though, because I remembered that Judy and Jr. had both talked to me like that right before they passed away. It was almost like they were unburdening themselves. Now Gene was doing the same thing. I could hardly hold my composure. Gene sensed that I was having trouble talking, and he said, "I'd better go back to the house. I'm getting tired and making too much noise. The deer will never come through." I helped him down the steps and asked him if he needed any help to get back to the house. He assured me he did not. He told me to stay there in case a big buck came by, and he got into his four-wheeler and I handed him his gun. The last thing he said to me as he started his four-wheeler was: "You go back up in the stand and get ready. There'll be a big buck passing through soon. See you later." Then he left and started down the path.

Crying unashamedly after Gene left, I went back up the steps and settled back in. I was thinking that my brother would not be with me much longer either. I tried to get my mind back on my hunting and started peering through the woods. All of a sudden, I heard a rustling noise. I looked closer and, just to my right, I saw a doe standing there. It was buck season, so I could not take a shot at the doe. But Gene's words echoed in my mind: "Where there's a doe, you will probably see a buck close by." Sure enough, I kept my eyes focused on the woods where the doe was standing, and a buck suddenly appeared. It was not too big, just a 6-point, but it was the biggest one I had seen in my 7 years of hunting. He was turned a little sideways and was very close to the doe, so I could not get a clean shot. Gene had told me to have a little patience and wait for my shot, and, just then, the doe moved away a little, just enough to give me a clear shot on the buck. I was nervous and the rush was there, but I took a good aim and BAM! down he went. I was so excited and away I went down to the house to tell Gene that I had gotten my first "real" buck. He was happy for me and reminded me that he had told me there would be one coming through. I wished that Gene had been right there beside me when I shot the buck but at least I had finally gotten my deer while hunting with Gene. Thank you, Jesus, for my hunting partner.

Buck season was over, and now it was time to get a doe. The day before doe season started, I went over to Gene's house to visit. We talked about a sundry of subjects, and there were some more things Gene wanted to say about himself and our life together. As we were talking, Gene got up and went into the other room and came out with a gun. I recognized the gun as being the one that my dad had given to him as a young boy. It had originally been our grandfather's. Gene handed the 12-gauge shotgun to me and said: "It's time to give this gun to you now. I've had it for a long time, and now it's your turn to keep it for a while." I was speechless, and I am usually not at a loss for words, as I took the gun from him. The gun had now been passed down for three generations. Gene told how this was the first gun that all three of us brothers had shot. It was sort of like becoming a man when dad let us shoot the gun. I was the last to shoot it. The gun is not in good enough shape to shoot now, but I will not have it repaired. I will leave it just like it is and then, when I am through with it, I will pass it down another generation. It was late, and Gene had fallen asleep. I went over to him and gently brushed his head. I told him, "I'm leaving now, but I'll be back. See you later." Then I walked out the door.

I visited Gene at Christmas time and later at his son's home, where he was staying. Gene was getting sicker and needed help going to the doctor and taking his medicine. His son's name was Gene, too, but we all called him Tiny, even though he is 6 feet 5 inches and weighs about 250 pounds. It was at Tiny's place where I visited with him on Sunday, February 20. My sister, Alice, and brother-in-law, Lloyd, were there, too. We had dinner together and talked about old times, as we often did when the siblings were together. Then, after dinner, Gene wanted to look at some deer hunting films. He had already seen them a hundred times, but he wanted us to see them, too. As sick as he was, he was still excited over showing and watching the video with us.

After watching the video for quite a while, Gene said he was getting tired and he went to his room to lie down. We had decided to leave then, so Lloyd and I went into his room to say our goodbyes. It was then that Gene asked, "Are you sure that I am saved and that I'll go to Heaven?" He told us he had done many wrong things and still wanted to make sure Jesus loved him and would welcome him into heaven. Even though Alice had led Gene to the Lord months before, we assured him again that he was saved* and we even went over the sinner's prayer with him again. After we were finished going over these things, he said he felt much better and was reassured. We all hugged and cried together. I left that day with a good feeling, knowing that Gene was saved.

On February 25, I got a call at work from Alice. She said that Gene was in the hospital and was failing. I immediately rang out my time card and headed for St. Vincent Hospital in Erie, Pennsylvania. I got to the hospital in 1 ½ hours and went right to his room. His children were already there, along with Alice and Lloyd. He was not able to say much since he was highly medicated and pretty much out of it. I stayed right by his side and was holding his hand when he passed away that evening.

I was surprised, once again, when his children asked if I would deliver the eulogy at his funeral. Although it would be hard for me to do this for another brother, it was an honor. In the eulogy, I told the people attending the funeral of Gene's love for hunting and his love for John Deere tractors. He loved his children and grandchildren, as well as his brothers and sister. He loved sports and played on several area softball teams. He also loved his white-faced Hereford cattle.

I also told about what Gene meant to me personally. I proceeded to tell the hunting story which I previously wrote about. He taught me so many things about life. He taught me a lot about mechanics, and this was a large part of why I got the job at Lincoln Electric. I was a millwright A at this company for over 37 years. Many of the things he taught me I used on my job there. He was always more critical of me than our brother, Jr., was but, later when I asked him about this, he said he was just getting me ready for life's trials and tribulations. It was the different kinds of nurturing I received from both of them that prepared me for many episodes in my life.

One particular incident I remember occurred when I was fifteen years old. He pulled his 1950 Olds off to the side of the road and told me it was time I learned to drive. Boy, was I surprised! The Olds was a nice car, and I never thought he would let me drive it. I did not even have a permit, since I was only 15. That was the first of many times I drove that car that summer and, about two weeks after I turned sixteen, I passed my driver's test on the first try.

Many, many people attended Gene's funeral. He was known throughout the community and had helped many people in his life. He was extremely mechanically inclined, and he was always helping someone fix farm equipment or motor vehicles. He definitely helped me fix my cars and trucks.

As we left the funeral home to head for the Edinboro cemetery, where he was to buried not far from dad and Gene's son, Russell, who had passed away a few years earlier, I looked back and notice that the cars were lined up for a mile or more. He probably had no idea that this many people cared. I owe so much to Gene and will miss him dearly. Thank you for not only being my brother and friend, but my hunting buddy, too. I love you, Gene.

CHAPTER 18

Richie

I have put this book together in chronological order, for the most part, with the exception of this chapter. I want to tell the reader about my special son, Richie. Richie was our first child, born just before Christmas on December 22, 1961, and his birth name was Richard, Jr. We all like to think of our children as being special, but Richie was special not only to me but to lots of people who met and came into contact with him. I could tell hundreds of stories about Richie but I will only share a few with the reader, at this time. Perhaps I will share more in a book about him at a later time.

One day I received a call from a friend of Richie's. He got right to the point and told me that Richie was at the square in Painesville and quite a crowd was gathering around him. Painesville, Ohio, is a small town just east of where I lived in Mentor. Like many Ohio cities, there is a square in the middle. Richie's friend did not seem to think that anything was wrong, but he thought I had better check it out. Even though Richie was an adult at this time I, like most fathers, got in my car and headed to Painesville to see what all the commotion was about. As I came upon the square, I could see a gathering of people in the northeast corner. I proceeded around the square and found a place to park. Then I saw Richie standing around some of the picnic tables, in the center of it all, with a bunch of other people. I literally ran across the square to see what was happening. I asked if everything was all right and what the problem was—all in one sentence.

Richie had a bunch of newspapers spread out on the table, like a tablecloth, and on top of that he had bread and packages of lunch meat, along with mustard and catsup. I said to him, "Richie, what are you doing?" He replied, "I'm just feeding some of my friends." Even though I am rather ashamed to admit it today, his response made me angry. I told him, "You can't spend your money feeding these people when you don't have anything yourself. Can't you see that these people are just taking advantage of you?"

I was very upset because Richie only worked part-time and for minimum wage jobs. He barely got by himself. The more I thought about it, the angrier I became. Richie said, "Don't yell, Dad. My friends are all watching and listening." I guess I had been embarrassing him. "I don't care who is watching or listening," I heatedly replied. I thought that might break it up and everyone would just go home. "You're feeding all these people, but how are you going to eat?" I asked. He explained, "I've already eaten today, and I have enough at home for the rest of the week."

He could see that I was still upset, as he calmly tried to explain things to me. "Remember when Mom passed away and we talked about the plans that Jesus had for us?" I nodded that I remembered, especially since Jeremiah 29:11 was one of my favorite Bible verses. "Well, this is the plan He has for me," he said. Then, without stopping, he quoted another favorite verse of mine—Matthew 25:40 "When you have done it for the least of them, it is the same as if you did it for me." I did not know what to say then. Richie was right. I guess I had taught him something that he remembered, all too well. He certainly did make me rethink my reasoning over again.

Boy, it is one thing for a dad to teach a son something, but this time the son had taught the dad something. In the next instant, I said, "Well, let's get to work, Richie. We have lots of people to make sandwiches for." That day, we made lots of sandwiches for Richie's friends and we all had a good time, eating and fellowshipping together.

That day was only the beginning of Richie's good works for the homeless. Years later, he received numerous plaques and awards for his work for the homeless. The News Herald placed a picture of him and a write-up about his work with the Harvest for Hunger food program in their newspaper. Richie volunteered hundreds of hours to these programs and the Salvation Army. As Richie later explained it to me, "I don't tell you how to spend your time or who to spend it with, Dad. But if it's okay with you, I would like to continue helping others." Of course, I could do nothing but agree with him. He had my wholehearted support, even though I did not always readily agree with his efforts. Richie spent many years donating his time to these selfless programs. There was no question in my mind that this was one of Lord's plans for him.

On May 30, 1997, I was called and told to come immediately to the Lake County East Hospital. Richie had been taken there, hyperventilating and having difficulty breathing. That was about 9:00 P.M. I rushed to the hospital and went straight to the emergency room entrance. Richie was in the first room where several doctors were working on him. They told me that Richie was not doing well and had been admitted, essentially, D.O.A. to the hospital. I frantically beseeched them to do everything possible for him. "What do you mean 'he's gone'?" I asked. "I see him breathing. Do something for him. If you can't do anything here, then let's transfer him to another hospital." One of the doctors answered: "You son would not survive even moving him from the hospital to the ambulance."

I kept begging them to help my son. They started some IV's and tried to do a blood transfusion. The whole time I kept talking to Richie. He was bleeding internally throughout his body, and the doctors could not stop the bleeding. I kept talking to him and, other than the breathing problem, it looked to me like he was going to make it. I had initially thought that Richie might have been in an accident or a fight, since he was black and blue over his entire body. I kept asking him what had happened, and he just kept saying that he was sick and had not been in an accident. I just kept trying to find out what the problem was, in case the doctors had missed something.

I then thought that maybe he had eaten something that was spoiled and had food poisoning.

Since Richie lived by himself, he did not always watch what he was eating. I thought he might have left something out of the refrigerator too long and it had spoiled. Or maybe someone had slipped him some kind of drugs in his food or drink. I was frantically reaching for straws, as his breathing became harder and the doctors seemed to have no answers.

My brother-in-law, Lloyd, had accompanied me to the hospital, so he was there with me in the emergency room. We kept talking to Richie and said many prayers. Lloyd would occasionally leave the room and I would continue to talk to Richie and he talked to me. It was the same type of situation as with my brothers and my wife shortly before they died. Richie kept talking to me, and we talked about everything. He began to have more trouble breathing, and his body was turning bluer than ever. The doctors asked me to leave for a little while. They put him into the intensive care unit room and then hooked him up to life support. After that was done, they allowed me to go back into his room to be with him.

Richie was now breathing better since he was on life support, but the doctors said he was failing fast. I was still able to communicate with him, and he said to me, "I'm not doing too well, Dad. It looks like I'm in a lot of trouble." I agreed with him and said that we were both in trouble. The last words he said to me were that he loved me and that the Lord had other plans for him now. He told me, "It looks like you're doing all right now and you don't need my help anymore. Just continue to do what the Lord has for you and I'll see you later." He then went into a coma and passed away a little while later. The doctors were able to bring him back after about 20 minutes, but he was never able to speak to me again. I stayed by his bedside all that night and at 9:00 the next morning he was gone. The doctors told me that he died from an extremely rare bacterial, infectious virus that caused severe internal bleeding and is almost always fatal.

I could not believe it! Twelve hours after I got the call saying he was in the hospital, he was gone! Those were the worst twelve hours I have ever gone through in my life. Lloyd had gone by then and my sister, Alice, was there at the hospital with me. Lloyd had been a tremendous help to me with his support and all the praying he did for Richie. He had not slept at all that night at the hospital before he had to leave to go to work. He did not want to go, but I convinced him to leave and thanked him for being there with me and for all his help and prayers. Alice was there with me now and that would have been what Richie would have wanted. Richie had been so close to his Uncle Lloyd.

Richie had helped so many needy people in his short life, and I was so glad for that. At his funeral, I was so proud of the fact that so many people got up to tell how Richie had led them to the Lord in the park on the square of Painesville, Ohio. What a wonderful blessing to know that Richie had been instrumental in leading so many to the Lord. I thought that I knew most of the people Richie associated with or came into contact with, but I was wrong. There were so many people whose lives he had touched whom I knew nothing about.

Then there were those people whom he knew very well who did not come to calling hours or the funeral. Neighbors who knew him since first grade did not come, a girl he had known and dated for a number of years did not come, and others who I really thought would be there to pay their respects did not come. I dismissed all these people from my mind, and concentrated and remembered the hundreds of people who <u>did come</u> to pay their respects to Richie. I will never forget all the homeless people who came. Richie surely had touched a lot of lives. He will not only be missed by his family and me but by the hundreds of others whose lives he touched.

Now that Richie was gone and since he had never been married, I was left alone and with no grandchildren. Richie was the last of the Richard L. Mook family. After I had lost my wife, my biggest concern had been to make sure that Richie would be taken care of. I had set up a trust in his name, but that still did not fully convince me that he would be taken care of. I guess I worried a little more about the situation than most fathers.

On the spiritual side of it, I know that Richie is well taken care of today and is not alone. Richie is now with Jesus, buried beside his mother and baby sister and where I will be buried someday. I have so much more to say about my son, Richie, but I am saving the rest of his story for another book. Richie had been a special son and he meant the world to me. He was only 35 years old when he passed from this life, but he did more in those few short years than most will do in several lifetimes. Many of the people whose lives Richie touched were young people placed in unfortunate positions, but who now, thanks to Richie, have many years to serve God.

When I gave the eulogy for my brother, Jr., Richie said to me: "Will you have some nice things to say about me like you did for Uncle Jr.?" I had not paid much attention to what he asked me at the time, and I sort of let it go in one ear and out the other. Little did I know that I would be giving my own special son's eulogy for him at this funeral. I am convinced that Richie will return to me and I will be reunited with him, now that he has done his duty here on earth. I know that Richie was not placed here on earth only for me to lose him, but he was put here to retrieve other lost souls. Richard, thank you for all you have done for me and all that you have taught me. You were such a good son. I will always miss you and you will always have a special place in my heart. I'll see you later. I love you. Dad.

CHAPTER 19

Stages of Grief

There are six phases of grief that I encountered and went through. The first phase for me was denial where I refused to believe that anything had happened. It is hard to believe that someone can just deny that a loved one has died, but it happens to a lot of people. Some of this has to do with the shock of it. It takes time to accept or even believe that a loved one is really gone. Even though a part of the brain acknowledges that a person is gone and is no longer there, it takes a while for everything to sink in and for our entire being to recognize that person is really gone. We feel like that person could come walking through the door at any minute. After my wife passed away, I would rush out the door at quitting time at work and jump into my car in anticipation of going home and then, all of a sudden, reality would hit and I would say to myself, "What's the hurry? She's not there waiting for me at home." What a letdown and a jolt. Let me say this, though: We can deny all we want, but it will not change anything. Our loved one is still gone and will not be coming back.

The next stage of grief I encountered was anger. Most grieving people eventually, if not right away, get mad at someone or something. I was no different. I got mad at many people, including God. I struggled with myself and God, asking Him how He could take so many people from me, the people I loved so dearly and were so close to me. I just could not understand how He could do that to me. I also became angry with the doctors and the hospital. My wife's illness had started out with a spot on one of her ovaries. It made sense to me that if the doctors removed both the spot and the ovary, my wife would be okay. The doctors had assured me that they had gotten all the cancer, but it came back anyway. Next, they performed a complete hysterectomy on Judy and, again, assured me that she would be okay. I believed them and, the next thing I knew, my wife was gone. I was so angry at the doctors and the hospital that I refused to pay the final bills that the insurance did not cover. I reasoned, "Why should I pay these bills when they promised to save my wife's life?" They did not keep their promise to me. However, after talking again with the doctors and the hospital, I finally made it right and paid the bills.

I was also angry at the pastor for only visiting my wife in the hospital one time. She had been in the hospital for 79 days, and he could only find time to visit her one time! He would not even perform her funeral service at the church or come to pay his respects at the funeral home. When I had asked him to preside at her graveside services, his replay was, "Let the funeral director do that." Needless to say, he was the target of my anger for a long time.

Of course, I was mad at some of the people in my workplace for not helping or understanding how devastated I was after the loss of my wife. However, there were many people who were empathetic and went out of their way to try to understand what I was going through. One person who really stood by me and helped me through this difficult time was Randy Taylor. He was the first person at my house when my wife passed away and I will never forget his steadfastness. He has remained a good friend throughout the years. However, there were, of course, some people who made my situation much worse by showing insensitivity and a spirit of not caring.

To top it off, I was even angry at my wife for leaving me alone. I had married her with the understanding that she would be with me for the rest of my life. Now where was she? I had ended up all by myself to face the rest of my life, with no partner by my side. I resented her leaving me all alone like that. I even experienced anger when Richie passed away because I felt that the last bit of my family had deserted me.

I could go on and on about who and what I was angry with during those times of loss in my life. It became so bad that I knew I had to get hold of myself and my anger, or it would kill me, too. The anger was only going to get worse if I did not do something to overcome it. So I will share with you some of the things I learned about dealing with the anger of losing someone.

I found that I had to voice my anger in some way, or it would have grabbed hold of me and never let go. If anger is not vented, most likely it will turn into depression. I had heard somewhere that the definition for depression is anger turned inward. That made a lot of sense to me. God certainly understands our anger, and we can always take it to Him to help us deal with it. Of course, talking with someone else about our feelings of anger is always helpful. We need to channel our anger into actions, maybe by doing something kind for someone else or helping someone. Somehow we have to let the anger go and replace it with something positive, or it will destroy us. I learned to express my anger by journaling, talking with others, and taking it to the Lord. The Lord always had time to listen to me, no matter how angry I was. After talking it out with Him, I always felt better.

Another common way some people deal with grief is bargaining, or constantly thinking about the "what-ifs." In other words, we want things to be like they used to be and keep asking, "What if...?" or "Why me?" If only I had done this or that, maybe this would not have happened. I bargained with the Lord when my wife was sick. I always prayed for one more day with her. I told the Lord, "If You will give me one more day with her, I will do this or that." I kept thinking, "What if I had gotten her in the hospital in December instead of January? Would it have made a difference?" What if I had not let Richie move out when he did, and he had stayed with me? Would he still be alive? What if baby Debbie had her crib in our room? We might have been able to save her. I worried myself to death with these useless questions. They got me nowhere, and only caused me more grief. Today, I am convinced that, even if things had happened differently, the outcomes would still have been the same. Even if I knew all the "why's" and "what if's," my loved ones would still be gone. It would not bring them back.

The only "why" I do not understand is this one: Why do bad things happen to so many good people? Entire books have been written about this very question, and no one seems to have any answers for this. I have thought it over and over and have come to the conclusion that it is not so much a question as a cry of pain and a reaching out for someone or something for comfort. We all want to be reassured in our hearts that we did the right things and that we did all we could do to save the person. In time, I have come to realize that I did the best I could under the circumstances. Once I came to realize this, I have been able to have a sort of peace within myself.

When going through the grief process, some people are more susceptible to depression than others. Depression should be avoided if at all possible. Grieving people should talk with others as much as they can, or go to a grief class. They need to talk with a pastor or a counselor. If needed, they should see a professional. I am thankful to the Lord that, even though I had my share of bad days and felt down and lonely quite often, I never went into actual depression where I needed professional help. Some people, I have found, do not even feel that they deserve to go on after the death of a loved one. I knew that the Lord wanted me to go on and that He had plans for me. Grieving people have a need and a right to tell their story. They need to share it with other people, especially other grieving people. We are all here to help each other through this difficult struggle called life.

Acceptance is another step in the grieving process. It goes along with denial somewhat. I describe it as leaving behind what needs to be left behind and bringing along what needs to be brought along. The sooner people can accept the fact that they have lost a loved one, the sooner they are able to get on with the grief process. I found that I could not run away from my grief. Oh, maybe I could for a little while, but I always had to come back to face it. I found that the sooner I dealt with it, the better. There is no time limit on the grieving process, and there is a different time limit for everybody. To be able to move on, people have to accept what has happened. They have to do it for themselves. I feel that people cannot move on with their lives until they have accepted their loss or losses.

In my case, I accepted the fact that my wife was gone. But I still did not understand what had really happened. After each of her operations, the doctors said that they were successful. I did not understand how they could say they were successful and reconcile it to the fact that she died a few months later. I felt so betrayed. This bothered me so much that, a few months after Judy passed away, I made an appointment with her doctor so he could explain to me what went wrong. He had told me that after each of the operations they had gotten all of the cancer and, just to be sure, they had put her through chemotherapy and radiation treatments. The doctors had felt she would be fine after all this. The operation had taken five hours and the doctor told me he would never have put her through all that if he had not thought she stood a good chance of surviving. He told me he had done the best he could under the circumstances. He point-blank told me: "I am a doctor, not Jesus our Lord and Saviour." That statement made it clear to me that he was only a man and had done the best he could. After talking with him, I was ready to move on.

Acceptance does not mean that all the pain is gone and that a person has to like what has happened. It means learning to hold onto God's hand and look to Him for love, trust, and hope. Acceptance is knowing that you are a different person now. It is the net result in a healthy grief process. I truly believe that the only way to start a new chapter in your life is to close the old one. That is just what I finally did.

Hope. The last step of the grief process is to realize that there is hope. I have found that death does not have to end a relationship. A lost loved one will live on in my heart forever. Do my loved ones want me to grieve forever? I know they do not. They would want me to go on in my life and remember that life is fragile.

During the grief process, a person has to walk in some low valleys before getting to the top of a mountain. Personally, I have been in some of the lowest valleys and I have been to the top of the mountain. I will be on top of the mountain again someday, but I have found that it does not take as long to get to the bottom of the valley as it does getting back on top of the mountain. The future is worth the expectation. I have not and will not waste the deaths of my loved ones. I have learned much from these losses, and I know that something good has come out of all this grief. God is our hope. My advice is to stay with Him and do not give up. Hope is for the future. In spite of all the losses, trials, and turmoils in my life, I have never lost hope or faith in the Lord. I still love the Lord.

Grief takes time. Do not have unrealistic expectations of yourself. Do not expect that, after one month, you should be at a particular place in your life and, after two months, you should be at another place and then, after a year, the grief will be all over with. The process is different for everyone. Do not compare yourself with others. Go gently and do not expect too much of yourself. Some days are better than others. Remember that you will get better. Take the time you need to grieve. Hold on to hope.

CHAPTER 20

Summary

You have now read about the nine closest people whom I have lost in my life. Of all these losses, Richie's death was the hardest for me to handle. He was my first-born, my only son, and my namesake. He was the heir-survivor appointment to the Richard L. Mook family. "Where do I go from here?" I asked myself. "I've been a long time struggling with my other losses, and here we go again."

In trying to find some of the answers, I have read many books and articles and attended seminars and grief classes. I have done a lot of praying and listening to others. While all of these things have helped me, I knew that I needed much more help from something more than doing these things. It was almost like, after exhausting every other possibility, I turned to the Lord more than ever before. I do not know how anyone could have handled the circumstances thrown my way without first being a Christian*, thus making it possible to turn to God for so many things and so much help. In this chapter, I will share some of the things that I have done to help me get over my grief. I have already shared part of the process of grief I went through. Now I will share with you some of the things I have heard, read, or experienced myself regarding grief and give you some of my own personal opinions on grief.

I have chosen to share my personal testimonies to inspire and help someone else, knowing that I have been blessed in spite of my grief. I now look forward to seeing what plans the Lord has for me, now that I have been able to retire after working more than 37 years for the Lincoln Electric Company. I hope the best is yet to come.

Although I had many tough years and trials while working there, I have to admit that I still earned a pretty good living at Lincoln Electric, working all those years without ever being laid off. That has meant a lot to me. The Lord answered my prayers and gave me a place to work, keep my family, pay my bills, and retire without owing anyone. He did not promise me, nor did I ask, for an easy place to work. All I asked was a place to work where I could make a good and decent living. That was exactly what Lincoln Electric did for me. I guess I have to think of as the glass being half full rather than half empty. I have to keep a positive attitude about the years working for Lincoln Electric. I have looked around and thought it over, and I realize that I have climbed many mountains, with many more to climb. I have accepted my station in life and have stayed the course, so I **can and will** finish the race.

I have told you where I have been in my life. Now I would like to tell you, in this final chapter, where I am today. I will tell you how I managed to survive all of the grief in my life and where I expect to be at the conclusion of my life. I will give you my takes on a variety of subjects and share with you some of the things that I did and things that helped me deal with my own grief. I hope this will be of help to you, too, even if you have not lost anyone or dealt with some of the hardships I have had in my life.

The biggest obstacle for me as I worked my way through my grief was the loneliness. It is hard for me to be alone, but the actual loneliness is the hardest part to handle. I never thought that being alone and loneliness would have two different meanings, but they certainly do. Let me explain.

I feel so alone at times. There were days when I was so down and I would have loved someone to call or visit, even if it was just to say hello. Sometimes I really did not feel like calling someone myself and, even if I did, I had the feeling that I was bothering them. People were always saying, "If there is anything I can do, please call me." Yet I did not feel they really meant it. There were so many times I wished that someone would call or visit, especially someone in my family. The loneliness really sets in, when you do not have callers or visitors. It seemed like no one really cared or understood the grieving I was dealing with. Of course, I knew that no one could really understand what I was going through, but I was hoping that people would have been more understanding and supportive. I found that family and friends seemed to pull back just when I needed someone to talk to and listen to some of the things I had to say.

I have family and some friends, but it seemed like others were wrapped up in their own lives and agendas. Everyone was busy and doing his or her own thing. So I had to learn how to live through my own grief. I also found that people will only listen to your grief so much and for so long. Then their patience with you is ended, and they expect you to get on with living. That is when I turned it all over to the Lord. I knew that He would listen to me for as long as it took to help me. He never got bored or impatient. He was never too busy to listen. The Lord always had time for me and never had other plans.

I have had many dreams, goals, and visions taken away from me through all my losses, but, with the help of family, friends, and the Lord, I have found that I can go through this thing called grief and come out a better and stronger person. That is just what I have done. I know I am a survivor. I have determined that the good days will outnumber the bad ones.

I had dreams of being married for fifty years. It was certainly a possibility, since we were married when we were quite young. All Judy had to do was live to be 67, and we would have achieved that goal. Alas, it was not to be. I had dreams of walking my daughter down the aisle and giving her away in marriage. Everyone in my family had done this with a daughter, so I expected to do the same with mine. Again, it was not to be. After losing both my daughter and my wife, plus having some health problems myself, I had dreams of Richie carrying on the Richard L. Mook name. Once again, the dream was taken away.

Not one to give up easily, I now have some new dreams. Retiring, writing this book, and eventually being reunited with my family in heaven are some of my new dreams. The retirement has been realized and writing this book has almost been realized now. It looks like most of my new dreams will come true. I will continue to dream my dreams.

To cope with my grief, I have made many changes in my life. My life is not the same as it once was, especially after the loss of my wife in 1987. I do not have the same friends that I once had when Judy was alive. Now that I am not married, I have lost many of the friends I had before. I never could really understand why some married people shy away from widows and widowers. I have my own opinions about this, but I do not have any real evidence to back it up. I can only make judgments based on my own experience and how things changed for me when I became single. I do not go out to dinner anymore with some of our old married friends my wife and I used to go out with. I guess they think of me as an "extra" now, a fifth wheel, the third person of a couple. Now that I am not married, perhaps my friends feel that I might be interested in their spouses. Even in a large group setting, being the only single person does not go over well. There always seems to be a little tension. I cannot explain it any better than that, but there is a change in the way married people treat me now that I am single. I am sure that not everyone feels the same way I do, but the change in how I am treated now is evident to me.

Even in an all singles' environment, I personally feel that there is a bit of a division between the never-married, the divorced, and the widowed singles. Many people do not agree with me on this, but it is what I have observed. I think that most people think that, after the loss of a spouse, a person will not forget that person easily. Therefore, a widow or widower's chances for ever having a good relationship with someone else would be slight, especially if he or she had a good marriage.

I keep many pictures of my lost loved ones displayed throughout my house and I am always receiving comments like: "Why don't you put those pictures away? They are gone now. The pictures won't bring them back." I disagree with these people. I cannot figure out what is so wrong with having pictures displayed of my son, daughter, brothers, and others whom I have lost. They will always have a place in my heart.

After I lost my baby daughter, no one told me that it was all right to grieve and that grieving was even necessary. I was bothered by comments some people made to me. Most of my family and friends felt that because we still had Richie that we would not miss Debbie. They would say things like, "You're young and can have more children," or "She was just a baby, so at least you weren't that attached to her." What unusual things for people to say! I am sure these people must have meant well and felt that these statements would somehow ease my pain. But they had the opposite effect on me. It certainly did not make us feel any better about the tragedy. It was also ironic that we did not have any other children and that Richie was gone now, too. With Richie's passing away, I cannot help but think that after I'm gone, it will be the last of the Richard Mook family. There will be no one to carry on my family name. Then, when I lost my wife, they said things like: "At least

211

you were married a long time (27 years)" and "You're young, so you'll probably get married again." When I lost my brothers, they would say things like: "At least you just lost a brother." With my son, it was: "At least you had him for 35 years." People always told me that I would get over it. I am not telling you these things to make you afraid to talk to people who have experienced a loss. However, I do tell you these things so you will watch and think about what you are saying to grieving people.

It was so hard for me to understand that, after losing my daughter, I had to go through the pain again of losing another child, my son Richie. One thing that all this grief has taught me, though, is how important it is to spend as much time as you can with your family, especially your wife and children. They should be the priority in your life; you never know what tomorrow might bring. I went out to dinner with Richie, and the next evening he was gone. I put Debbie to bed one night, and the next morning she was gone. Even though both my brothers were sick, the same thing happened with them. I went hunting with my brother Gene one month, and he was gone the next month. I visited with my brother Jr. on Sunday, and he passed away the next Wednesday. I thought Judy was coming home for Christmas, and twelve hours after we had been talking about everything she was gone.

My philosophy now is that I will never look back on my life and say that I wish I had mowed the lawn more often, or I should have washed my car more frequently, or I should have painted the house one more time, or even that I should have gone to work more often. I could go on and on, but I think the point is made. What I do wish is that I had spent more time with my family and friends. The chores and duties of life will always be there waiting for you, but family and friends will not always be there.

I have gone to my shop's Quarter Century Club banquet 13 times and, after talking with some of the retirees, I have never heard one of them say that he should have worked a few more years, especially the ones who retired after 60 years of age. I realize today that for many years I foolishly wasted my time on things that were only temporary, things that are as dust and quickly blown away.

I have taken so many things for granted in my life, like my wife having my dinner ready when I got home from work, my clothes always washed and cleaned, the house clean and orderly, and thinking my wife would always be there for me. I took for granted Richie being there to help me in the yard, to talk sports with, to go to ballgames with, and on and on. I took it for granted that he would be here long after me and had even set up a trust for him with everything I had in his name. All of that changed in the blink of an eye. Most of us know this at some subconscious level, but we do not make the changes in our lives that we should. We do not prioritize the time spent with our families. We think there is always tomorrow and we constantly procrastinate. I say, Do not count on there always being a tomorrow.

Life can never be the same after the loss of a member of a family, but the Lord does promise us that our lives can be good again. He does not promise that they will be the same, but our lives can be good and fruitful. We have to do our grief work (and, believe me, it is work), and we have to give ourselves time. As far as I am concerned, there is no way around this thing called grief. A person just has to go straight through the grieving process.

I can assure you, though, that we do not have to go through the grieving process alone. I have become closer to the Lord than ever before. Feeling that no one else understood my grief, I turned to the Lord for sustenance. He was always there to listen to me and speak to me when there was no one else. When the chips were down, He was always there. He promises us in His Word that He will never leave us or forsake us. He has certainly kept this promise to me.

Like in the Footprints poem I received in the hospital during my open-heart surgery, He says, "My precious, precious child, I love you and I will never leave you." He was the one I could turn to. I have had to put my trust in the Lord and go on with my life, even though going on was one of the hardest things I have ever done. Knowing that God cares certainly does help, but even that does not take away all the hurt and sorrow. I still have to go on.

HOW FAR IS HEAVEN?

LADDER OR STAIRWAY?

The way I understand it, once we get to heaven all the pain, hurt, suffering, sorrow, and tears will be gone. I have been very fortunate in knowing that all my family has been saved and are in heaven. I have accepted the Lord as my own personal Saviour and am trying my best to serve the Lord, so I know I will see them all again. It all sounds so easy and, to be honest, it is. How thankful I am that, even though I have lost so many in my family, I have the assurance that I will see them again. As I stand before the Lord at the Eternal Reunion, what treasures will be waiting for me in my new home.

How far is heaven? It may seem like it is many miles away and out of reach, but, let me assure you, it is not that far away. When I was growing up as a youngster, I could visualize getting the extension ladder and climbing it rung by rung until I reached heaven. At that time, I wanted to see my mother and it seemed realistic to me that I might be able to get to heaven to see her that way. It was not farfetched for a little kid to think this way. We are just passing through here on earth and heaven will be for an eternity. In Matthew, the Lord said, "I have gone on before you and prepared a mansion." I have seen some beautiful homes here on earth, but they do not even come close to the one He has prepared for us in heaven.

If you do not know Jesus as your personal Saviour, I encourage you to invite Him into your heart and life now. Jesus has already chosen you, and now it is up to you to choose Him. It has always amazed me that Jesus has the most recognizable picture in the world, but people do not really know Him. Do you know Him? Now is the time. As you are reading this,

I would encourage you to stop and accept Him as your Saviour. Right now.

My losses have caused me to search more and more for solace within the pages of God's Word. The Bible is a never-ending resource of beloved verses which have supplied me with meaning and comfort over the years. One of my favorite verses is found in Jeremiah 29:11 -"For I know the plans I have for you, declares the Lord, plans for a future and a hope." To know that the Lord still has plans for me, even after all my losses, inspires me and gives me reason for living. My world was all monkeyed up and it was hard for me to believe that God could have plans for someone like me. I soon found out that he had wondrous plans for me. However, they were not the same ones I had. Let me explain.

I never planned on being a facilitator at a grief workshop, let alone being one of the featured speakers. I certainly never dreamed I would be going to other churches to speak on the topic of grief. I never planned on delivering the Sunday morning message from different church pulpits. I definitely did not envision being the master of ceremonies at my company banquet and telling 1500 people in attendance about what the Lord meant to me. In front of them all, I thanked the Lord for the opportunity of knowing Him and telling the audience that the Lord had already chosen them, too, and that now all they had to do was choose Him. I have to believe that no one had ever made statements like that before at a company banquet, but I felt the Lord was leading me to do so. Last but not least, I never thought I would write a book and share my personal testimonies in it. I could go on and on about the plans He has for me, but He has plans for you, too. Just like, as you have read, He had plans for Richie, too.

In Isaiah 57:1,2 we read: "The good men perish, and the godly die before their time." This verse tells me that God has taken some of my loved ones away now, maybe so they will be spared from the evil days ahead. "For the godly who die shall rest in peace." This verse tells me that something worse could have happened to my loved ones, but now they are with the Lord and doing fine as He watches over them. I take great comfort from these verses.

Another comforting Bible passage is Psalms 34:17,18 where it says: "The righteous cry out, and the Lord hears them. He delivers them from all their troubles. The Lord is close to the brokenhearted and saves those who are crushed in spirit." This tells me that God promises that He will always be with me. All I have to do is call on Him and He will hear me and answer me. He wants to be my friend forever.

In other comforting verses, the Lord says, "I will never leave you or forsake you." God says, "He will supply all my needs and give me peace and understanding." The Lord says, "Don't be afraid. God is still upon the throne. I will help you." God will give us peace and rest. He knows just how we feel. He tells us, "Come unto me, all ye that labor and are heavy laden, and I will give you rest." (Matthew 11:28) We do not ever have to face the world alone. We do not ever have to be afraid. What blessed assurance!

We have to ask, seek, and knock, as it says in Matthew 7:7. "Ask and it will be given to you, seek and you will find, knock and the door will be open to you." I have asked and it was given. I have sought and I have found. I have knocked and the door was opened.

What is on the other side? Earlier, I told of having open heart surgery. It was at this time that the door was really opened for me and I got a glimpse of the other side. I was ready to go in and the Lord told me: "Not now. I have other plans for you." Oh, what a beautiful sight it was. I could go on and on with sustaining Bible verses. Each verse may have a different meaning for each person. I truly encourage people to read their Bibles.

I was on vacation in Yellowstone National Park after a huge fire had destroyed thousands of acres in that beautiful area. The park ranger told a story about inspecting the fire damage and finding a dead bird in a clump of ashes. He went over to the ashes and moved them with his boot. To his surprise, four little baby birds jumped up and flew away. This story reminds me of Psalms 91:4 where it says: "He will cover you with His feathers and under His wings, you will find refuge." That is exactly what He did for me during those days when my grief was almost more than I could bear.

God tells me that He has gone on before me and already prepared a mansion for me. All I have to do to claim my mansion is to knock on the door, and it will be opened. What a meeting that will be, just to touch the hem of His garment and to reach for His hands with His arms wide open, welcoming me. These were a few of the Bible verses that really helped me.

I have found that, after going through so many losses in my life, most people just have no idea what to say. Even when they did try to express their sympathy in some way verbally, it came across as insincere and insensitive. I am sure that people mean well, but they do not always think things out before they say them. Some of the things they said were quite hurtful. Sometimes the less said, the better. If you do not know what to say, just a gentle touch or a little hug is worth a thousand words. It seemed that, after each loss, fewer and fewer people had anything helpful to say to me because they were so afraid of saying something wrong. I have to admit that people just being there for me was a big help.

It aggravated me that most people, especially those who have never lost anyone extremely close to them. Believed that the grieving process was only for a short period of time and that you had to somehow put it all behind you and get on with your life. In fact, many people became quite impatient with me when my grieving did not fit in with their perceived time frame. I returned to work a week after my wife died. The first day after I returned, I was not doing too well. I was having trouble concentrating on my work and the tears would come quite easily. The boss saw me when I was moping around, rather tearful. He did not ask me how I was doing or try to help me in any way. Instead, he wanted to send me home, not because of my grieving, but because he felt I was not being productive enough and getting my work done. He told me that I was dwelling on my wife's death and was setting a bad example for the other workers. He did not want them to see me like that.

Eventually, there was a meeting of the heads of my company and they decided that I was grieving too long. I attended the meeting and I asked my boss straightforwardly: "How long do you think the grieving process for losing a wife should be?" He said without hesitation: "About a week. You had a week off, now it's time to get back to work. If a week is not long enough for you, then stay home until you are all through grieving." If my boss's opinion were the right one, then I would still be at home grieving. I still grieve for my lost loved ones to this day.

In our society, working men and women are not allowed to grieve. They are given a few days off for the funeral and are then expected to go right back to work as if nothing had happened. Even if more time off is given, the grieving person still feels the tremendous responsibilities of work and the bills that still need to be paid. People are not given the amount of time they need to grieve or the support they need while they are grieving. I remember my boss saying, "Real men don't cry." I responded with, "Are you kidding? I cry over a lot less than losing my wife!"

While someone is grieving, I cannot emphasize how important it is to take care of your health. It is so easy to neglect yourself. Make sure you watch your diet and get plenty of rest. After my wife passed away, I lost a lot of weight. I was too heavy anyway and needed to lose some. However, I did not realize how little I was eating until I had lost 65 pounds. After I

RICHARD L. MOOK

lost my son, I did just the opposite and gained the 65 pounds back. Whenever there is loss, there is tremendous stress. Sleeping too much or too little is not the right way, either.

About a year after I lost my son, I suffered a heart attack. The loss of my son, stress in the work environment, poor eating habits, worrying, and resting properly—all were contributing factors leading up to the heart attack. I cannot emphasize enough how important it is to take care of yourself. Now, every so often, I take a day for myself. That day I do something just for Richard. I may go to a special place, or buy some little thing, or maybe just go to nearby Lake Erie to watch the water and the boats passing through. Maybe I will take a book and read to escape for a while from everyday stresses. Whatever I do that day, I do just for Richard.

As if my losses in themselves were not bad enough, when they happened on or near holidays or days of importance, it seemed they were ten times worse. My mom died on the same date as President Kennedy, November 22, even though she died quite a few years before. Judy died in December near Christmas. Debbie was born at Thanksgiving time, but my brother, Jr., died at Thanksgiving. My brother, Gene, died February 25 and Debbie died February 24—37 years apart. Richie passed away on Memorial Day. All of these sad days have something to do with the holidays and, thus, it makes holidays that much harder for me to endure.

I have always loved music, and I have turned to some of the lyrics of songs for help. One of my favorite songs is "It Is No Secret." This song was one of the first songs I learned to sing as a young boy. It was a hit tune, for both the religious and secular worlds. I think it was ever number one on the music charts, and it has been recorded by several different musical artists throughout the years. The song was first written over 50 years ago, but the words still have a powerful impact on me. The words in this song are not in the Bible word for word, but the central meaning of them is.

"It Is No Secret" has been a favorite of mine for a long time. Some people think it is a secret what He can do, but I think I really know what the secret is. I will share what I think this secret is if you promise to share it with someone else. The secret is: You cannot always depend on others for help or depend on others to make you happy. But I have found that God, in all His wisdom, will take care of you. He has done it for others, and He will do it for you. He will take care of you, all the while with His arms wide open, and He will pardon you. I have seen what He has done for others, and I know He will do it for you and me. Why? Because He promises us He will. If He said He will do it, then that is good enough for me.

In my grief classes, I have met many people whom the Lord has taken care of as He promised. I could tell story after story of the wonderful things He has done for people in my grief classes. People have remarried, had more children, gotten better jobs, written poems, sung beautiful songs, written books, facilitated grief classes, gone to college, and made other major changes in their lives—all when they felt their lives were already over. But, most importantly of all, I have been a witness to some who have accepted the Lord as their Saviour. That is why I say, as the song says, "He has done for others, and He will do for me and you."

Another song I always loved which became a number one hit was "One Day at a Time." In this song, Jesus says that you have to take it one day at a time. You will not heal or your grief will not go away in a day or two. You have to continue on, one day at a time. Sometimes the pain will get worse than before, but the Lord says to hold on and eventually it will get better. We are to ask the Lord to help us in our belief and show us the stairway we have to climb. Yesterday is gone and tomorrow may never be yours, the Lord tells us, so we have to ask Him to give us the strength to do what we have to do. We have to remember that God has walked this path many times before. Who else better to turn to than One who has gone before? In Matthew 6:34, we are told not to worry about tomorrow, for tomorrow will take care or itself. Each day has enough trouble of its own. Once again, take it one day at a time.

"Because He lives I can face tomorrow" are lyrics in another song that means so much to me and is so true. I don't know about tomorrow, but I know who holds my hand. Those words certainly helped me get through some great difficulties, and I am sure they can help you, too. He will hold your hand, just as He did mine. He is never far away from you at any one time, and all you have to is extend your hand and He will hold onto it. There is nothing like having someone hold your hand to comfort you in time of need. In my opinion, it is not because He lived and died so much as He died and now He lives.

"He's the lily of the valley," the song goes. Not just the lily of the valley, but the lily of my valley. When I was way down in the valley where it was nearly impossible for flowers to grow, He brought sunshine to enable me to grow.

"Though dark may be night, all I need is a ray of light to help me with the trials I go through." These were words in a song that Pastor Yeary used to sing at the Lakeshore Assembly of God Church, located in Mentor, Ohio. That song always touched and spoke to my heart.

Last but not least, "The Old Rugged Cross" was a favorite of Judy, Richie, and me. This song was sung by all in attendance at both of their funerals as a tribute to them. I hope that it will be sung at my funeral, too, someday.

All of the songs I have mentioned have touched me in a special way throughout my life. These great songs have helped me deal with my grief. I now have a new song, not only to listen to but to sing. A song of praise and thanks, so that others will hear of the glorious things He has done for me, especially how He has led me from grief to glory. Remember to listen to the music, for the song is going to end. I am determined to continue to sing my songs.

Even though I was saved at the age of 12, I was aware that the life ahead of me would have many difficult trials and that I would encounter many problems in life. But I never in my wildest

RICHARD L. MOOK

imagination thought these trials would occur to the degree they did in my life. I sometimes think of Job and all the roadblocks along his way. I saw how God took away everything he had, but he still remained faithful to the Lord. That was encouraging to me as I faced the trials in my own life. I always had to remind myself that God would answer my prayers as, time and time again, I would ask Him for help and guidance in my life.

I certainly do not have all the answers as to why my life has taken all these twists and turns or why I have had to deal with as much grief as I have. But I have clearly seen that God can use these circumstances for His glory. Through all this grief, I can tell you that the Lord has been good to me and I have been blessed beyond any words I can write here. Through some of my talks in different classes and churches, I feel blessed to have been instrumental in leading someone to the Lord. I had never dreamed that, through my talks or writings, I might help lead someone to the Lord. There is no bigger thrill on earth. Oh, what a blessing this has been for me! It confirms for me that God has other plans for me, too, just as Richie had always told me.

I am here today because God preserved me. He had other plans for me and people prayed for me. Part of the reason for writing this book was the belief that I had suffered through all this grief for a reason. I knew there had to be some meaning in it all. Now I know that helping others going through the same grief was always part of God's plan for me. God wants me to show people that, no matter what the circumstances, they can overcome this thing called grief, too.

Many people say that moments do not mean anything. But, as you can see from reading about my life, your dear ones can be taken away from you in a moment, without any notice. Are you ready for this to happen? Not 99 percent, but 100 percent ready? Now is the time to make things right with someone. It could be your last chance.

I keep thinking about what my family would want me to do, now that I am left alone. Would they want me to just stay home, looking out the window as the world passes by? I know that they would not want this for me. The world keeps right on going, despite my losses, and it certainly is not going to wait for me. As my family looks down upon me from heaven, I know they want me to move on. I hope they are saying, "We may be gone, but you live on and we do not want you to give up. We know the Lord still has plans for you." I often think about where I might be if the Lord had not passed my way.

I have made many mistakes in my life, and I have told you about some of them. I hope that by reading this book you might not make some of the same mistakes I did. I do not expect you to substitute my way of thinking for yours, but I hope you are able to keep an open mind and think about some of the things I have shared with you in this book.

I want to thank again all the people who have helped me throughout my life. There are too many names to mention them all in this book, even though I have mentioned some. I sometimes talked about some of the people who did not help, but many people contributed to helping this poor little farm boy go FROM GRIEF TO GLORY. A special thanks to our Lord and Saviour for watching over me and never leaving me. Thank you for always being by my side and close by, especially during my trials and tribulations when I did not always follow You the way I should have. Thank You for never giving up on me, though it seemed like, at times, I gave up on You.

I still do not understand why all my loved ones left me so soon. It would be difficult to get close to someone again and then maybe lose that person. I lived by myself at age 15 and was alone. I think that experience helped me to grow up a little sooner and prepare me for all this a little bit. However, that experience does not come close to the feelings of loneliness I experience on some days now. I keep reminding myself that all the loneliness will go away when I walk the streets of gold with my family. I have a home in glory land. He has prepared a mansion for me and is waiting there for me. There will be no more pain, tears, and suffering. I look forward to meeting Jesus at the door of Heaven and to touch the hem of His garment. Oh, just to have a closer walk and talk with Him, all the while being reunited with my loved ones. I have a lot of catching up to do. Yes, the best is yet to come.

NOTES

Most Bible verses are taken from the King James Version and the New International Version.

Saved: Means to admit that one is a sinner, to repent one's sins, and to receive Jesus Christ as one's Lord and Saviour.
Christian: One who has determined that the direction of his life will be toward Jesus Christ, not away from Him, and one who is fully committed to that way.
Poems: "Footprints" and "The Letter" apparently have authors who are unknown.

Some sentences and one-liners are taken from Bible verses, poems, songs, and sayings by others.

ABOUT THE AUTHOR

The author, Richard L. Mook, was born in rural Cambridge Springs, Pennsylvania, and, after moving at about the age of ten, was raised on a farm near Conneaut, Ohio. Despite growing up under poor economic conditions and many dire circumstances, he graduated from Rowe High School in Conneaut and attended Lake Community College in Mentor, Ohio.

During and after losing his nine closest family members, Mr. Mook turned to God for help and understanding. He decided, after retiring from the Lincoln Electric Company in Euclid, Ohio, with 37 years of service, to write this book with the hope of helping others going through similar circumstances. Along with writing, the author also speaks at various churches, delivering a message of how God has led him from grief to glory. He now resides in Mentor, Ohio.